# How to Live
## on the
## Planet Earth

Nanao Sakaki

# HOW TO LIVE ON THE PLANET EARTH

COLLECTED POEMS

BLACKBERRY BOOKS     NOBLEBORO

Some of the poems in this book were previously published in *Bellyfulls*
(Toad Press, 1966); *Real Play* (Tooth of Time, 1981); *Break the Mirror*
(North Point Press, 1987); *Break the Mirror* (Blackberry Books, 1996); *Let's
Eat Stars* (Blackberry Books, 1997). We would like to thank the presses,
their editors, designers, & all involved in getting Nanao's poems to print.
The later poems have been gathered from many sources. Many thanks
should go to Studio Reaf for long support of Nanao's life & work. This book
is dedicated to the vast lifelong network of Nanao's friends & family.

Illustrations: Nanao Sakaki, *ink on paper*

Cover photograph: Courtesy of Gary Snyder
*Suwanose Island, 1967—Nanao Sakaki singing*
*with Shinkai, Satsuki Kano, and Kaya Yamuda*

Back cover photograph: John Suiter
*Nanao Sakaki reading at Yoyogi Park, Tokyo, Earth Day, 2006*

Frontispiece & endpiece photographs: John Suiter

Inside photograph: Nancy Fisher
*Gregroy Corso, Allen Ginsberg & Nanao Sakaki,*
*Santa Fe, New Mexico, June 1972*
Courtesy of the Allen Ginsberg Estate

Coda photograph: *Beth Leonard*

Book design: JB Bryan / La Alameda Press

ISBN 978-0-9824389-4-7

Blackberry Books
617 East Neck Road
Nobleboro, ME 04555
chimfarm@gwi.net

# Contents

# Foreword

NANAO SAKAKI IS WELL KNOWN IN THE LITERARY CAPITALS of the world as a uniquely free and bold-spirited wanderer, occasional river or mountain activist, singer and chanter, and internationally published poet.

These images are a congenial surface to his life and work. The life of this lean, dark-tanned man spans from a childhood in militaristic pre-war Japan, World War II (in which Nanao served as an Air Force Radar Analyst); the Japan of post-war poverty and the long slow recovery; with the recent emergence of Japan as an economic powerhouse and environmental Godzilla. Throughout these years he has developed a grand sense of nature, dissected the workings of social systems, and kept a steady focus on craft and art, that his poetry might play a role in the evolution of an alternative culture. His small but potent body of work is unlike any other. Many strategies: mind-leaps in scales of time or space; an exquisite attention to the tiny; the use of astronomy, geology, and ecology; all woven into inventive poetic stories and dramas.

Grounded and plain, with surprisingly sweet reversals (as in "Valentine") he can then turn to pitilessly excoriating our very selves, down to their skeletal remains ("Autumn Equinox") as a way of asking, "what's it all for?" Nanao looks into the scary otherworlds and invites us, as the skulls invite him, to cross over ("Travel Light")— and maybe this then earns him the right to write a few poems of outright instruction, how to live—which always have his surprise slant —useful indeed. As, "How to Live on the Planet Earth." There are elements of such delicious surprise in these poems that I am boggled when I reread them. How did he come to wish Copernicus a good sleep? Wish Allen Ginsberg so light-hearted a farewell? Meet his lover as a falling walnut?

Some poems bring forth the language of science, as Nanao unself-consciously goes about his studies: watching for the planet Mercury at sunset ("Goodnight Copernicus"). He makes "information" work in poetry, playful but serious with the aptness of his well-won knowl-edge. Who ever wrote a long poem about the planetary ecology of toilet paper before? For the bold, there is ever new territory.

Nanao recently told me that none of the poetry of Japan much interested him. "Except" he said after a moment's thought, "imayo." Imayo, which means "present-day songs", were a type of popular song during the Heian Era (8th to 12th centuries)—many little lyrics on the themes of longing, loss, the quest for wisdom—and witty and gentle images from the lives of young gamblers, strollers, and lovers. Grim as a few of his poems are, there is always humor. Nanao also praised the *Kanginshu* songs of the Japanese Era of Wars, *Sengoku jidai*, saying, "They are quiet songs. The people kept singing them, even during the terrible turmoil."

There is indeed an old folksong quality embedded in many of the poems, and in some an echo of the voice of Japanese country vaude-ville, *manzai,* or the quirky tone of the rustic *kyogen* comic can be heard. Nanao sings and chants with a deep melodic resonance, which is recorded on the several CDs he and his musician colleagues have made. Nanao once said that he read (in the fifties) how a *San* (Bush-man) elder told Laurens van der Post "There is a dream dreaming us." This, for Nanao, was a crucial "turning phrase" that set him to study-ing the world of Primitive and Ancient cultures. Nanao's poems are tuned to the basics.

Many of Nanao's poems use strategies of cumulative repetition, and have the flavor of oral literature with its riddles, sayings, fables, and formulaic devices; little ways of unfolding narrative that go back millennia. Childlike, playful, goofy and immediate, his poems none-theless remain serious, adult, and propose strong medicine: "Break the Mirror!" of the small self.

Nanao has also written three plays and has usually been personally involved in their community production. He says he writes plays not so much for the audiences as for the people who want to act in them. "Everybody likes plays, they are sociable, and everybody wants to be an actor or actress, everybody is really acting, every day."

One time Nanao said "'*kokorozashi*'—that's what's in my poems. It's something from the Chinese Middle Ages. It's from medieval Japan. It means, the spirit of determination, confidence, vision, intention—a will to change things." This has the tone of the Robin Hood revolutionary wilderness-dwelling guerrillas of medieval China described in the Chinese epic novel *Shui Hu Chuan,* "The Water Margin."

One of my sons once asked, after Nanao had stayed with us a round of days and moved on, "How does he manage to live like that"? Nanao has walked many a literal mile (both in Japan and on Turtle Island), and has burned the lamp late as he pored over old books. His life has seen a heap of hard knocks. Nanao's life and work has been "edited by Hunger and Cold; revised by Cold and Hunger" (As Hakuin says of his own Commentary on the *Shingyo*).

Nanao generally lets you know by mail if he is heading your way. Then you'll hear him singing from afar, as he walks up the road. He opens his backpack and brings out good maps, a good notebook, a real pen, and often some local field guides. Sit down by the fire, drink tea, talk of the latest journey. Eat, and he always helps clean up. Drink some spirits, and people get convivial for hours. Nanao brings reports from the cultural front lines of Asia or New Mexico or Manhattan. And next day we go for walks together, or work in the garden, thin green apples, stack firewood. Some imitators have tried to follow in his wayfarer's footsteps and found it wasn't easy. Same for his writing.

These are internationally fluent free-verse poems that actually do have the right to be called "post-modern"—poems that have survived the angry dreams of both right and left politics. Within their deep root of old vernacular culture, old song, is a sophisticated vision of "future primitive"—a poetry something like that. The gift of Nanao Sakaki.


## NANAO

Gleaming smile

Big heart

Strange loneliness

Long view


*Gary Snyder*
NIGHT OF THE PERSEID METEORS, 1998

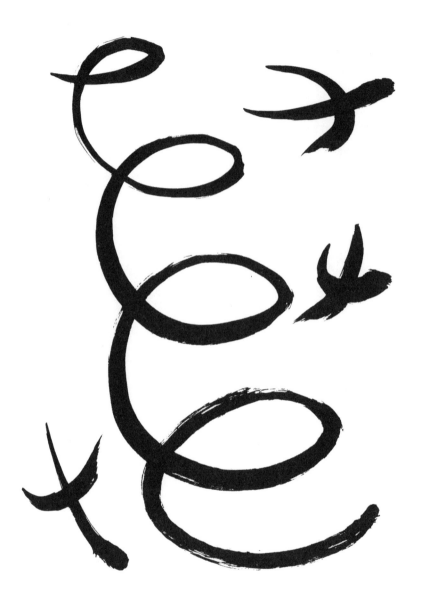

# BELLYFULLS

# Bellyfulls

# I

"I love you" feels the darkening window dummy's rough powder-snow mixed with a white wink, passing under seven-waterfalled-breast with—in the night—the spreading sound of all-or-nothing rapids, following charred rockskin scarring fingertips, Mary's lover leads a suffering ass and opening tobacco-reeking fly YAHOO!

It is, but because the semicircles are misunderstood the dance-floor stumbling slopes on tongue and semen vehicles of lies—why is the smouldering stump of virgin green rain frog before a sudden shower, turns horizontally around the upright teastalk chipped from sun, end of umbilical hoard of labor pains, dwells only a thousand up from slaves in front of stations of commercial law and body height, whores lengthening dazzling lightning flash begonias nose, impaling hope-smeared grubs on sticks for food—

All the climate of misprint, so one day with sea parted stiffening crane is tangled in hard bread of hungry souls and bamboo-grass of debts, the irritable col hooks on the steps of mistweed, dull alibi stallion withering, cairn's crumbling townful buildings while the tail of constance trembles on a lizard does not bend a hundred years—

  mountain stream of idle conversation rainbow avalanches sperm on alpine roses crimson week, counting clock-tick falling stones, lifting healthy third leg long the toothmarks of cruel crampons on a butterfly, over-diagonal model globe goes bankrupt in stiff constipation and the cut thread of a previous offense

  disturbance arc continues in abundant turpentine for freezers full of loving couples, naive magnet pointing south, a cubed expression depths from physiology, turns round steam turbine stam-

mer drumbreast throbbing in big sister's kite on string, gouging
yesterday out of the blackhead of a tomb,

comparing lengths of burnt-out butts that chant the
finger-ordering "haiku" worn out retirement brush as blossoming in
the spray of a heat-haze, to approve the milky way shaft drowning in
Pachinko lava and, caterpillars image of the shiver-and-echo
twittering fossil state of human love,

Rumbling brassband of the moon's spear takes
off nightless widows weeds and is the vale of tears rains down from
diapers soluble in pawn-forfeit heroes dangling from cracked mainmast
responsibilities and the median line death penalty—so saying you with
dynamite in mouth love nakedness . . .

—AT OKUCHICHIBU

# II

Under the four rainy seasons what are you? scaly ferns
growing from prominent navels rotting permanent waves
hurrying up the hypotenuse of a squall split from the gray and
pubic-hairless sly on big-bellied women vipers in long raspberrying
shaggy banyans of black breasts, and the twin thunderclap of crystals
and great cedar felling dear weather coming out in weals

Pre-Old Testament angle of elevation twine about the
cold and beautifully naked passion fruit splitting open on forest
crosses first flow, sentinel rocks of others, dolmen of the stiffening
flying-fish at fire-site onion peels and missing leaves whirling and
spreading out on horse face in its everlasting jungle of weekly
magazines

And the next in the regular service of sampan and
pork-soup's chopped up gramophone record of flypaper fuzzy in
the ears of the dormouse burning with intestinal worms—this is
mankind!

The hill of greening banana-boy's virginity piling up
in drops of dialect musty as the far-off asthma of the nightingale,
standing on the blood group of rhododendrons, hinds that wet
their pants upright, rough-textured placenta of public-opinion-and-
typhoon-winnowing granite, the lie of rich sugar-content spraying
on the one-price-only daydream dimming illegal opera glasses root
strike in ghostly tropical grass, astrology continuing as split second
bargain counter speed of cheap hips more vertical than the devas-
tated cliff's afterglow of burning stakes of cannas in the suspended
sentence summer

Playing card permutations become a melody which wills
shame on itself in sluggish comb dried mackerel pieces, washing

the ultra-violet rays and the primary-colored angry string of islands parasites on white-of-egg of conscience,

      Why shouldn't you exhausted cotton waste in swamp of fallen trees stay the perfectly mannered speed of sound at peeling off the skin of salary?

      Because of phosphorescent insects warming up of memory the wind velocity of mossy mushroom in the mask of a rusted mirror is twice solidifying lens and stratus cloud, so with surrounding sea and vault of heaven all yolk of egg—between us and the annual rings of the flowing plural menses———

        —AT YAKUSHIMA

# III

In slacks of bones because of chewing cows please
spread ticks tangled in saliva stingy octane-rate great colts feet on
Y-junction of the sulphur smelling new moon clouded creeping
pines and summer solstice striped mosquitoes full of blossom

And wait for me where the murder rate is in full
flower on steps of cumulous while I, next to the mountain stream
of crow and squint, wind up the rocky hill piled high with brown
bears spring dung curling in the snow ravine rear mirror

Cut across the northern latitude horned owl who
loves to rip the transient leaves gas smell suburban manners and
false teeth of Brocken avalanching down sound bell in alpine birches,
feel the twitching veins of wolves who hasten in unison their own
weathering,

Swallows' delta welcome news, agglomerate standing
out distinct from Fohn triangular waves, line up on elephantiasis
benches overhanging shelf erased potassium stain,

Bum the seal zigzagging up the meeting tides, the
red rose is over-made-up on the carpet snow, heaped up ponytails
waterfall behind the heel of my self-portrait fall in sleet on border
only obtuse-angled prison terms of drift-ice pile-up balancing
accounts. . . . .

—AT HOKKAIDO, THE SHIRETOKO PENINSULA

# IV

Stand up snakes! Bursting the basting threads
twined on betel-palms, you, leaf-veins of hungry panties on the
desperate banana tree, sliding down the papaya trunk sliced-up
sail you stake your life on, in loess scorched by high interest keel
of random rainfall stopping your ears to the star-and-anchor
menacing reef and roar of breakers summer orange a burr in the
throat

Caught on chest hairs of star coral bloodshot from
camellia, wolf-in-sheep's-clothing stones on roofs! baring defiant
bums the momentary crimson bank deposit always glaring from
the cliff of square of monkeys and the pantomime, in a forest of
pygmy ants turned rosaries on the necks of dummy flowers that
nod yes yes to neon

Waiting vine of false morality and watermelon
physiognomy, greasy with the mascara ofcycads and yawns,
eruption should the bougainvillea culminate,

Take off bare feet of "harmony"—noodles whirling
on the wave crests of a cherry blossom snowstorm even pigs can't
bear—camphorized bridal night swimming through rice fields of
inflammable heat,

After warm palm-vomiting current, northern limit
of pimp traitor to the world's time deviations.

*Translated by Neale Hunter*

# # 101

Emerald sky
Leprous sea
What wretched dreams I'm dreaming!
Always mooring a sampan—

I hope to get free of
Timidity just now breaking out,
Stripping myself soul's nappy,
It's a bargain.
At the end of a scene with your ghost
I went up the ravine
Came back thru New Year's spitz-smelling
Charred pile caressing evening calm.
Then spongy future peers
Into the morning mist of "honeyed words"
But you can jump over it as crickets.

Eternity is supper for sows.
I myself Jack
Ate an overflowing silence in summer time
Pubic hairs of human history.
Devour a damp crater plus the placenta
Sink to the lake at mid winter
Sleep to satiety.

There goes Xmas party of mice in the kitchen
There goes singing of ardent spirits on beach
There comes vomit to the eardrum

There comes a blizzard merrily
Happiness calls back
Bellyfulls of falling stone.
Let's have coffee, business and creed.
False red peppers come down silently
To the time table.
But you can smile if you could
Next is scabby calendar,
Tore off a sheet, it says "I love you"
Take care of French pox in a crescent moon.
Naked teacher, misery carrier-pigeon,
A tower clock in a park
You and your stone image are going down to the sun.
Artificial flowers, or jets of waters, perfumes.
Hey skylark, higher and higher!
—you may fall down to heaven—

If you want to love something
It could be the wind of Greek letters
Or tomb of duty getting sober
Once more    ding-dong
A chimpanzee is the very image of grandfather,
Namby-pamby footprints,
Over there boiling hamburgers
Narrow lane of spherical clusters.

*Translated by the author*

# REAL PLAY

If you have time to chatter

Read books

If you have time to read

Walk into mountain, desert and ocean

If you have time to walk

Sing songs and dance

If you have time to dance

Sit quietly, you Happy Lucky Idiot

# Nice Meeting You

Underground deep
fossil cave      dark

you sit down
might be midday

someone comes in
you can't see him, hear him, touch him

still someone with you for sure;
is he      friend or devil?

you don't care
all the same

you smile
he looks blank
I burst into laughter

no body
wave after wave

# Urgent Telegram

Everything starts from Miso soup,      good morning!
Miso soup is made of shiny spider web
Life begins with Amazon ocean
Grand Canyon ends with God-like Odysseus
His great grandson shall be Dharma bum
Your great gran'ma shall be rattlesnake
Rattlesnake is seed of meditation
Meditation seed of pumpkin pie
Pumpkin mother of sacred mushroom
Mushroom father of God
God grows with galaxy
Galaxy is a stolen diamond
Last night my turkey vulture ate it
Tomorrow I fly to high glacier.

# Sunshine Orange

sunshine orange, brilliant beach cirrus colored
remote from toil, remote from singing, remote from prayer

sunshine orange, brilliant beach
wrecked boats rotting, sandals rotting, sea wrack rotting,
wild rose rotting, mermaids rotting, fire works rotting
soap bubbles rotting

Milarepa breathing

monksfood-flowers rusting, a torpedo rusting
rusting raven asleep, the Giliaks asleep, Ezo wolves asleep
the pygmy fairy asleep, the saber toothed asleep, mammoth asleep
dinosaur asleep, Poseidon asleep, submarine-volcano asleep

seagull's circle dance dreaming high
Indian blue sky spinning
sea current. Big Dipper spinning
sunless heaven spinning
raven dark
Mother Earth, Gran'ma Rock
fallen over the precipice
Shuko shines with her bloody smile
that towering rock broken off last year by
drifting ice—flaming clear like her
where is the debris?
far from Tierra del Fuego, far from Nepal
far from Shakyamuni, far from Hong Kong flowers

beyond the end of thundering
a thundering rainbow

sunshine orange, morning-glow beach salmon pink
a stray fox kit cries in the woods
last night a hermit crab
crossed over the channel, border
the sun walks in Libra today
a wagtail chases a hawk

Universe the ocean of Eternity
Eternity, the beach of Peace
Peace, near a cascade in the canyon
between sea-rumbling and ear-drumming
bouncing sound bouncing rock

sunshine orange, brilliant beach cirrus colored
remote from toil, remote from singing, remote from prayer

sunshine orange, life's beach, sunshine orange.

# A Sand Painting

On a coral sand beach

Plumed egret's footprints.
Little ringed plover's footprints.

On a beach rock
A blue rock thrush's morning song
                *"chu-i-ri chu-i-ri chi chi"*

A gathering of Hermit crabs
who love their commune so much.

These huge footprints are mine?
                *"chu-i-ri chu-i-ri chi chi"*

Every footprint is a song
                the song of life
                painted on the sand
painted in the air . . .

                *"chu-i-ri chu-i-ri chi chi"*

FEBRUARY 22, 1976  *Iriomote, Okinawa*

# Sharpening a Knife

Nanao, keep your knife clean
Nanao, keep your mind clean

Sea breeze is bad for a knife they say
Sea breeze is good for a mind they say

Sea breeze not bad for a knife
Sharpen your knife, that's all

Sea breeze neither bad nor good
The ocean a whetstone for mind

A clean knife mind
A clean mind ocean
Nanao, sleep well tonight
Blossoming crinum lily as a shelter
The coral sand beach as a bed
The Southern Cross as a pillow.

# An Axiom

After evening glow
Jupiter shadows the coral reef

I am part of human beings
Human beings / mammals
Mammals / animal kingdom
Animal kingdom / all creatures
All creatures / earth
Earth / solar system
Solar system / Galaxy
Galaxy / whole universe
Therefore, I am a part of the whole universe

Dark midnight
A water rail sings in a mangrove

I am equal to human beings
Human beings / mammals
Mammals / animal kingdom
Animal kingdom / all creatures
All creatures / earth
Earth / solar system
Solar system / Galaxy
Galaxy / whole universe
Therefore, I am equal to the whole universe

Before daybreak
From unknown depth
To the coral reef
Rising up spring tide
ah      Love!

# Prime Numbers

At dawn
Set out to the north
   rucksack on my shoulder

       in East China Sea
       on a coral, mangrove ringed isle

A brief storm
       running running running

       Breaking morning
       Breaking spring
       Breaking myth open

1 plus 1 equals
    2.3.5.7.11

MARCH 1976 *Amami, Japan*

# A Love Letter

Within a circle of one meter
You sit, pray and sing.

Within a shelter ten meters large
You sleep well, rain sounds a lullaby.

Within a field a hundred meters large
Raise rice and goats.

Within a valley a thousand meters large
Gather firewood, water, wild vegetables and Amanitas.

Within a forest ten kilometers large
Play with raccoons, hawks,
Poison snakes and butterflies.

Mountainous country Shinano
A hundred kilometers large
Where someone lives leisurely, they say.

Within a circle one thousand kilometers large
Go to see the southern coral reef in summer
Or winter drifting ices in the sea of Okhotsk.

Within a circle ten thousand kilometers large
Walking somewhere on the earth.

Within a circle one hundred thousand kilometers large
Swimming in the sea of shooting stars.

Within a circle one million kilometers large
Upon the spaced-out yellow mustard blossoms
The moon in the east, the sun west.

Within a circle ten billion kilometers large
Pop far out of the solar system mandala.

Within a circle ten thousand light years large
The Galaxy full blooming in spring.

Within a circle one million light years large
Andromeda is melting away into snowing cherry flowers.

Now within a circle ten billion light years large
All thoughts of time, space are burnt away
There again you sit, pray and sing
You sit, pray and sing.

# Right Now

1978 May 11th 9pm Thursday
Rainy, fresh breeze, C 18 degrees

Jugon sings Kenji Miyazawa's "Against rain"
Mr. Muddy plays bass guitar
Percussion Toshi and Saka
Back from Grand Canyon.
Guitars Koppe and Meibin.
Tape recording Satan and Lumper
Jugon's two daughters sleeping
                      holding each other.

          "This is Tokyo"
Once upon a time poetess Chieko Takamura cried
          "There is no more sky in Tokyo"
Rainbow photo on to-day's front page.
          "Very unusual"
Japanese government says
          "we dispatch rifle corps to the New Tokyo Airport."
more news
          "without oxygen bottles
               two Austrians
                    climbed Mt. Everest."

# Ladies and Gentlemen!

why too many things in the world!
most of them, nonsense, ugly, crazy.
when I go to supermarket for fish bones
I'm shaken by so much poor stuff to see.
most striking
beyond my imagination,
TOILET PAPER.

signs of life, droppings on animal trails,
hi coyote, hi deer, hi grizzly, hi skunk!
to buy toilet paper, I wonder,
& Tokyo salamander*
must go to Tokyo every week for toilet paper?

eat like a bird
sleep like a fish
by the mystery of mammal
I pay tax to nature,
every early morning
without toilet paper.

in a clear running brook
sending off my old food
I clean the bottom with fresh water.

by locality and season
light works on fairies in many ways,
form, color, smell—

tender and sweet for your ass.
hi morning glory, hi camellia, hi magnolia!

the land of eagle,
Pinacate desert, Mexico.
cleansed by a barrel cactus flower
buried deep into volcanic sand
oh, my old old stuff
now it may bloom
as a flower of yucca, the desert candle.

oh grass! oh tree!
you goddess of oxygen, energy, beauty!
indifferent to man's infidelity
you are generous with
flowers in spring
green in summer
scarlet in autumn:
hi sage brush, hi juniper, hi cottonwood!
don't tickle my anus, hi soma the mushroom!

ladies and gentlemen!
at sun rising
gather rainbow dew
on the broad leaf of taro,
exorcise your buttocks.

gunpowdered ghost skull of trees,
infernal factory kicks out pulp—paper
pile up, heap up, high up in supermarket
TOILET PAPER

it's coming
a flood of toilet paper
like diarrhea
together with all creatures
the flood will carry us down into Hades.

heaven's tapestry—
our flying sisters' feathers,
spread lavishly
in woods, beach, prairie and city,
lovely for your cleansing,
hi hummingbird, hi winter wren,
hi roadrunner, hi common egret!

coral bouquet of ocean,
but don't use live polyp,
it surely hurts your bottom;
dry seaweed, cowrie shell, O.K.

if you like (an octopus arm).
charmed by your droppings in shallow water
small fish come to you
catch them, eat them for mercy.
whale the great
hi MobyDick
wash my tailbone with your spout!

backbone of Mother Earth,
Y junction of eternity, human history and your soul,
the most gracious lavatory paper
rock and stone!
hatched by sun
in a creekbed

this opalescent pebble
breathes, grows and goes
to the other shore with us.
so sweet, so warm!
can you buy such a cute one in the market?

here in glacier
wind mind freezing
nothing available as tissue paper, but
look! passing over the moraine
a patch of white cloud.

ladies and gentlemen!
it is high time.
I must pay tax to the earth.
along limpid stream
canyon azalea starts blooming today.
crouching on a tiny waterfall
listening to a dipper's song
the flower in my hand
I meditate upon a happy shit,
perfect ceremony of universal circulation
so ancient
so fresh day by day.


* *Tokyo Salamander—Hinobiidae nebulosus tokyoensis*

# One Two Three Four

There is no human kind
        but . . . you!

There is no nature
        but . . .

        one
        two
        three
        four thistle flowers blooming
        in the evening breeze.

SUMMER 1978 *Elk Valley, California*

# Memorandum

1970:      Carlsbad Caverns, then I moved to
White Sands National Monument.
Dr. Albert Einstein
government officials and the Pentagon
all watched
the mushroom-shaped cloud
right here in the Chihuahua desert
25 years ago.

1973:      Jemez Springs, New Mexico,
I met a Christian priest.
At Tinian Air Base in Micronesia
he held a service for "B-29" pilots
who headed for Hiroshima,
August 6, 1945.

1945:      Izumi Air Base in Yaponesia
100 miles south of Nagasaki.
Three days after the Hiroshima bombing
a "B-29".
Due north. 30,000 feet high. 300m.p.h.
Three minutes later
someone shouted,
"Look, a volcanic eruption!"
In the direction of Nagasaki
I saw the mushroom-shaped cloud
with my own eyes.

1946:  Hiroshima. There,
       one year after the bombing
       I searched for
       one of my missing friends.
       As a substitute for him
       I found a shadow man.
       The atomic ray instantly
       disintegrated his whole body.
       all—but shadow alive
       on concrete steps.

1972:  Bandelier National Monument.
       Beautiful ruin
       of ancient people, the Anasazi.
       Dead of night, the earth
       quakes three times.
       Not by Jemez volcano
       but by underground nuclear explosion
       in Los Alamos.
       More ruins, more churches!

1975:  The Air Base ruin in Yaponesia,
       south of Nagasaki.
       No more "Kamikaze pilots,"
       now 3,000 cranes soaring high
       in the setting sun.

1979:  Northern edge of Chihuahua desert,
       Bosque del Apache National Wildlife Refuge.
       Sandhill crane, "Grus canadensis": 1,700.
       Whooping crane, "Grus Americana": none.

As a substitute
for the extincting species
Mr. Kerr-McGee wants to dump
ever-existing nuclear waste
into "The Land of Enchantment."

# A Trail Song

Good-bye to mosquitoes, horseflies and desert fleas
I walked back from the Rio Grande
To a plaza in so-called "Old Town" in a growing city.

High noon—dry, hot, breezy.
Airplane contrail melts into blue quickly.
Over Sandia Crest a thunderhead bubbling—
Robins fly over adobe souvenir shops.
Cottonwood seeds snowflake.

> Under a green shade
> sitting on a white bench
> I wonder what history is.

Street names in Spanish, French and English.
Two cannons from the Civil War
Cast in nineteenth-century Boston—
Distant rock'n roll, church bell. Apache trail song.

Cars move counter-clockwise around square.
Police, beggars, restless tourists—
Pale-faced women, big-bellied men,
Kids shouting, running—
From the plaza, few miles southeast
Manzano*/Apple/mountain hides
Death seeds in its core.

An old lady
With a sheep dog,
Smiles, "Writing poetry?"

Gentle breeze
History breathes

Which trail to take?

* *Manzano mountain—East of Albuquerque, New Mexico,
where the military stores outdated nuclear weapons.*

# Summer Morning Song

On a summer morning
    Walking in Japanese mountain woods
        A sixteen-year-old boy
            I met my first love—

This round-faced girl
    Slim body, sharp-rayed
        Gold eyes—not really shy—
            Liked me to look at her
                Dressed up green just for me.

We met in a high meadow.
    I called her "Mountain Lady"—
        Behind a thorn fence
            Watching her lips blooming
                In summer morning light.

Crossing many many winters, gray-headed man
    Finds his way to a new continent
        Walking woods in southern Rockies
            With another summer morning light
            I meet my old love.

She's still sixteen-years-old as before
    With a round face and edible root—
        A native yellow south Asian plant.

What a traveler walking east to Japan
    Wandering west to the Rockies
        Without fear, without feet.
            From my mountain lady's golden face
                Shine out beauty, intelligence and patience.

No beginning, no ending to love
    Whenever summer blooms back over earth,
        We meet in a high meadow . . .
            Weaving fuzzy globe of star-seed cluster
                Waiting for another summer to glide.

Don't call my lady
        "Oyster Plant."

# Me, a Caterpillar

On a dirt mountain road
Our old truck moves through half-green forest.

    "Last summer a great many caterpillars
    Ate away the whole forest greens.
    But good rains in spring—
    Greenery is coming back slowly."

A little later the driver mumbles
"Where are the caterpillars now?"

A memory, all of a sudden,
Flashes in my heart.
Several summers ago
I passed this road with somebody.

    Smells of sage, flowers and dry air.
    Snow-capped peaks, rainbows, lightning
    A face, a smile, a voice—

My heart bumping along the bumpy road.
"Where'd the memory come from?" I wonder.

    Me, a caterpillar
    Eating the greens of life
    Leaving debris of memories
    Carrying shaggy dreams into nowhere—

On a sudden turn in the road
Thunder claps in my spine.

# Future Knows

Thus I heard:

Oakland, California—
To teacher's question
An eleven-year-old girl answered,
"The ocean is
A huge swimming pool with cement walls."

On a starry summer night
At a camping ground in Japan
A nine-year-old boy from Tokyo complained,
"Ugly, too many stars."

At a department store in Kyoto
One of my friends bought a beetle
For his son, seven years old.

A few hours later
The boy brought his dead bug
To a hardware store, asking
"Change battery please."

# Wind Speaks

When in doubt
Tell the truth—Mark Twain

When in pain
Listen to wind.

These black oaks
As Paul Cezanne draws
Stand slanting in morning wind.

It's the day of Hiroshima, August 6.

I hear my Neanderthal man's bone
Rattling with wind.

# All Over the World

London tower of nightmare.

New York mental hospital.

Tokyo slave market.

Los Angeles ghost town.

Kalamazoo, Michigan

    one of the first American cities to close streets
    for a pedestrian shopping mall.

Taos, New Mexico

    construction of
    a giant supermarket commences.

Taos Mountain

        an idiot
        sits on a lotus flower
        all day long
        in a tipi.

# Halloween '79

Snowstorm over back mountain—
Bear's footprints on the trail—
Without sound
Crows fly over the tipi.

> There      is
> No   Magic   Land
> No   Magic   Time

> You
> Are
> Magical.

Your      eyes
The setting sun.

# Why Do You Write Poems?

Because my stomach is empty,
Because my throat's itching,
Because my bellybutton's laughing
Because my heart is love burning.

# Top Ten of American Poetry

The United States themselves are essentially
                    the greatest poem.—Walt Whitman

The government of the people, by the people,
                    for the people. —Thomas Jefferson

You deserve a break today.—MacDonald's

Where science gets down to business.—Rockwell International

Kick the letter habit.—Bell System

Crime hits everybody. Everybody oughta hit back.
                    —Chicago Crime Commission

Without chemicals life itself would be impossible.
                    —Monsanto

I think America's future is black, coal black.
                    —Atlantic Richfield Company

Have a coke and a smile.—Coca Cola

Private property—No trespassing—Dead end road.
                    —Anonymous

# Two, Four, Six, Nine Bunnies

in the morning
I find two newborn bunnies . . .
a white, a black
in a cage near my neighbor's tipi.

in the evening
I ask Dan,
"Did you see two bunnies?"
"Yes, but four."
I return to the cage . . .
there . . . six bunnies!
two white, two dark brown, two black

the next morning
Carol comes back from the tipi.
"Nine bunnies; I'm sure!"
I hurry to the cage, wading in deep snow.
Yes, nine bunnies . . . two white, a gray
two light brown, two dark brown, two black.

innocent eyes . . . moving jewels!
tiny, tiny mouth.. .wonderful appetite!
they already start nibbling half-frozen lettuce.

they grow quick until big enough
to be eaten by man.

man grows slowly until big-bellied enough
to be eaten by death god.

death god grows very slow until oily enough
to be eaten by everlasting fire.

        . . . no escape at all?
        . . . yes!
        . . . how?

        wriggle out of your cage!
        burst out of your big-belly!
        gulp down the death god!
        jump over the everlasting fire!

couple of days after
I find two bunnies lie frozen
a white, a black
        . . . eyes never open.

# Firewood

Looking for firewood in snow mountains

Carrying back firewood
  Splitting firewood
    Listening to burning wood
      Watching for dancing flame

      So joyous
        You forget yourself
          You forget a serious appointment
         You become a piece of firewood

        Warming up
        Flaming up
        Singing up
        Dancing up

        You become ash.

# Enlightenment

——As no end in the universe I have no shadow in my mind.

——Impossible!

——Sure, yes!

——I wanna' catch your mind's tail.

——Without tail who can dance?

JUNE 1980 *El Salto, NM*

# Supper

Sundown—
>Clouds blazing
>Wind running
>Birds crying.

A gigantic evening glow—
>Stay with me
>My brother. Summer!
>Your light, your heat, your soul!

Transient crimson sky—
>The flavors of life
>Sweet, sour and bitter
>All melt into the dark.

Summer solstice—
>Vega, Altair, Deneb
>Calling stars

>John, Nancy, Mary
>Calling friends

>I boil bracken's fiddleheads
>—Supper for everybody.

# A Message

The crescent moon sets
      Star light
      Wind light
      Lightning

From the Galactic center in Sagittarius
      A mosquito
      On my nose.

# Forevergreen

*For Issa*


Ten years ago
In a new town outside Tokyo
Housewives wanted seriously
To have green stuff in their yard.
But trees shed leaves—much trouble.
So they planted evergreen plastic trees.

Four hundred years ago
On an autumn morning in Kyoto
Rikyu, the first tea master, asked his son
To clean the tea garden.
After the son swept and reswept all fallen leaves,
The master shook a maple tree.

One hundred fifty million years ago
In a Jurassic valley
A dinosaur drowned in a bog.
Time transformed him into fossil oil.
Then, God metamorphosed him into plastic.
In Tokyo he now stands, a tree, never shedding leaves.

A dry, windy summer day
I climbed White Mountain, east of Sierra Nevada,
To chant for a Bristlecone Pine,
Four thousand six hundred years old.

A warm rainy spring night in south Japan
I slept under shelter of a Yakasugi tree,
Seven thousand six hundred years old.

From a sunspot
A young tree starts growing today.

# Autumn Equinox 1980

Blow out your candle!
—I see the stars twinkling.
Blow out the stars!
—There, lightning.
Pick off your eyeballs!
—sweet-heart-ocean-waves sounding.
Pluck your ears!
—I smell of honey, milk, and wine's river.
Cut off your nose!
—Kiss me please.
Shut your mouth!
—My skin breathing, touching, talking.
Take off your skin!

> Muscles, intestines, all your bones
> Hanging upside down
> Homo Sapiens Sapiens

> In a meat market
> In a megalopolis
> In a great century.

> How much money
> Would you pay
> To have your body back?

# All's Right with the World

Monday morning
Nobody in my house.
Visit next door,
Nobody there either.
Call the police.
Phone rings three minutes—no answer.

"Frankenstein" on TV tonight.
God's in His heaven—
All's right with the world!

Tuesday morning
No dogs, no cats, no mice in my house.
Visit next door,
No dogs, no cats, no mice there either.
Call the pet hospital,
Phone rings three minutes—no answer.

"Charlie Chaplin" on TV tonight
God's in his heaven—
All's right with the world!

Wednesday morning
No bugs, no fish, no birds in my yard.
Visit next door,
No bugs, no fish, no birds there either.
Call the zoo.
Phone rings three minutes—no answer.

"Marilyn Monroe" on TV tonight
God's in His heaven—
All's right with the world!

Thursday morning
No flowers, no vegetables, no trees in my garden.
Visit next door,
No flowers, no vegetables, no trees there either.
Call the nurseryman.
Phone rings three minutes—no answer.

"La Dolce Vita" on TV tonight.
God's in His heaven—
All's right with the world!

Friday morning
Mountains and rivers are gone.
Drive to a nearby city.
No mountains, no rivers there either.
Call the Federal Government.
Phone rings three minutes—no answer.

"Star Trek" on TV tonight.
God's in His heaven—
All's right with the world!

Saturday morning
Our planet, the mother earth, is gone forever.
Call my psychiatrist
Phone rings three minutes—no answer.

> "Shogun" on TV tonight,
> God's in his heaven—
> All's right with the world!

Sunday morning.
God walks back to church,
Says, "Good morning"————no answer.

# After the First Snow

From the ground
     snow comes.

To heaven
     sap goes back.

At the end of universe
     life starts.

In the wind
     time walks.

# Grasshoppers

Hi Fred!
You don't want to have
Vegetable garden this summer, do you?

————No, too many grasshoppers.

Why don't you eat them?

           ————Prairie Shrimp————!

Catch them with butterfly net
Take off legs and head
Saute in butter
Eat with garlic and soy sauce

Next morning
Give your shit back to the garden;
Now with numberless grasshoppers

           Sing songs
           Hop
           Jump
           Dance
           Forever

# Why

Why climb a mountain?

Look! a mountain there.

I don't climb mountain.
Mountain climbs me.

Mountain is myself.
I climb on myself.

There is no mountain
            nor myself.
            Something
            moves up and down
            in the air.

# Please

Sing a song
or
Laugh
or
Cry
or
Go away.

# Vinegar

With vinegar
I clean up windows.
I clean up mind's windows.
I clean up green forest blue sky white clouds
I clean up great universe.

————not true————

Now transparent windows—

Against the glass
Chickadees, robins, jays
hit their heads
and lose their lives.

In charity
I pick them up
    eat them up
    with friends.

# Winter Flower Trails

After two days snowing
A rosy evening glow.

You remember suddenly
The star shining in daytime
And flowers blooming here in summer.

Star light
Snow light
An icy thistle field.

Staggering with heavy boots
You break dry flowers
Into small pieces of the sun.

Start here
Your footprints
Animal tracks
Flower trails.

Shine over the zodiacal light
Along the Milky Way.

# Money Means

Toys, Blood, Sweat
Salt, Manure, Money, Hookworm
Number, Pebbles, Star dust.

Toys for kids
Blood for the poor
Sweat for laborer
Salt for fisherman
Manure for farmer
Money for snob
Hookworm for the greedy
Number for the rich
Pebbles for snail
Star dust for angel.

Star dust, Pebbles, Number
Hookworm, Money, Manure, Salt
Sweat, Blood, Toys.

# Midday

A gray shadow
Crosses over snow field.
A white cloud
Floats in blue sky.
Between heaven and earth.
Between you and me
Light dancing.

MARCH 1981

# False Solomon's Seal

(1)    Much eating makes stomach-ache
    Much knowledge head-ache
    Much sensibility mind-ache
    Much thinking heart attack

(2)    To know is to get lost.

(3)    Go to the ant,
    Thou sluggard
    Consider her ways
    And be silly like her.

(4)    Money makes the horse go
    Honey makes the bear walk
    Irony makes man run away.

(5)    Give the tutor to an idiot
    Give the dictionary to a scholar
    Give a graveyard to the dead
    Give the cake to me.

(6)    The early bird catches the worm
    Spare eater the wisdom of belly
    Jolly worker the wisdom of mind
    God the wisdom of silence.

(7)    Birthing————for this encounter
    Old age————sky blue turquoise

Sickness————life so rich
Death————let's go to bed.

(8)     Even though
        Even though
        I love this wrecked earth
        $1+1=1$.

(9)     The sky is always blue
        The moon always full
        The sea always high
        You always complaining.

(10)    In a strange country

        If you want to know the land
                Learn the weeds.
        If you want to know the culture
                Check the craft.
        If you want to know the future of the land
                Listen to the folk music.
        If you want to know the people
                Know yourself.

# YAPONESIA
# FREEWAY

# Twinkling

Stars twinkling
Breeze twinkling
Christmas tree twinkling
Leaves twinkling
Frost twinkling
Earthworms twinkling
Mary twinkling
Peter twinkling
Nanao   twinkling
        twinkling
        twinkling
        twinkling
            twinkles

# Fade Away

Fade away the star trail
Fade away the wind trail
Fade away the water trail
Fade away the bird trail
Fade away the butterfly trail
Fade away the animal trail
Fade away the man's trail
Fade away everything
        How about you?

# Wanted

Stand high on the horizontal waves,
  The Southern Cross!

Nonchalantly fly over the sacred air,
  Coronet eagles!

Endlessly celebrate your dark mountain sanctuary,
  Wildcats!

Cover the world over,
  The green of mangrove!

Resound with the sea—rumbling,
  Bob's morning song!

Hold the setting sun steadily,
  You, Hera's unborn baby!

Wanted—a water buffalo
    a fishing boat
    a jamisen
    a loom
    And you!

# Seven Lines

If it rains, you could be wet;

If a gale comes, you could blow away;

If you have a mouth
    you can always get something to eat;

When you have hands, you can work;

When you have legs, you can go;

You have a voice, why not sing?

You have a heart, dance!

# Clock

typhoons, floods, together with ridiculous exploitations.
soundless, continuous landslidings on our mountain.
drinking viper-flavored Sake
I listen to an old man's story
of our exterminated sister mammals;
flying squirrel, river otter. Kappa or river monster
and Yamanba or mountain witch.
my eyes stick to strange, shiny, black stuff
winding around the old man's wrist.

digital watch.
no dial-plate
no minute-hand, no hour-hand, 1 2 3 . . .
1 2 3 4 5 6 7 8 9 0 1 2 3 . . .

soundless, continuous landslidings in these days.
typhoons, floods, together with ridiculous exploitations in Japan.
wars, massacres, together with ridiculous exploitations in the world.
now, a future glacier fills up all valleys over the earth
with scratches of the miracle of numeral, digital computer.

salary, house rent, monthly installment, tax, debt, fine,
blood pressure, pulse, life insurance, mortality life insurance,
pet graveyard payment, car license number, postal code,
telephone number, passport number . . .

digital watch.
no dial plate

no minute-hand, no hour-hand,
no eyes, no nose, no ears,
soundless, continuous landslidings 1 2 3 . . .
1 2 3 4 5 6 7 8 9 0 1 2 3 . . .
glacier now fills up

all valleys of the earth with digital scratches.
winding around the wrist of Erect Numeral Man
strange, shiny, black nail marks.

under the fast sinking autumn sun
picking my way through tricky gorge
following shiny fringed wild pink flowers as daytime lighthouse
I hurry back to the old farmhouse.

under the crimson glow of sunset
dirty-nosed boy, mamma and myself
now eat mountain crystal clock, the Akebia fruits
together with seeds
together with eternity.

# No Trespassing

Fine, blue, autumn sky over my head.
It's a good day for mushroom hunting.
Along the trail
Touch-me-not and asters full blooming.
Merrily my legs walk up,
Merrily my mind jumps up.

Halfway to mountaintop
There stands a hand painted wooden sign:
>"No trespassing in search of wild mushrooms.
>If you commit an offence
>You pay four hundred dollar fine."

Cat's cradle of mycelium—
Mushrooms trespass on all color, smell, taste of life and death.
Here in narrow corner of limitless fungus world
Man makes a bare living.
Without cultivating by hand
He steals beauty and strength of mushrooms.
Driven by greedy motives
He always gets entangled in spider web.

Walking downhill
Clearing spider webs
I almost step on cluster of maroon fairy
On dead oak stump.

Hold your palms open always! Rucksackful of fungi now:
Brick cap. Boletus edulis, Caesar's mushroom. No artificial poison,

no fertilizer — perfect natural foods.
Everlasting blue of the sky.
Limitless wealth of the forest.
I write new signboard in my mind:

> "Welcome to the mountain!
> Pick up anything you want!
> If you love mushrooms,
> You are already a billionaire."

# Stinkbugs

1. Insects will conquer the human world soon.
   —Right now many insects openly invade my house.
   The first; Silverfish with white armor, thread-thin antennae.
   These dwellers of bookcase slum
   Nibble my books, great jewels of wisdom,
   One by one, day and night.

2. Haiku poem by Issa:
       "There must be parent and child like us
       In a school of running Silverfish."
   One morning I killed eight mercilessly.
   A nightmare—Silverfish's fertility in east Asia.

3. The second; Hitler bug or Yellow jacket.
   High up on wall of my humble cottage
   These wasps built a castle—
   Gorgeous, Renaissance style.
   With horrible sharp spears
   They threaten my honorable guests.
   Someday, I'm afraid,
   My free, healthy, peaceful, elegant life
   Might be destroyed by their merciless attack
   Like an unlucky beehive.

4. The third; Scot's stinkbug, *Monida scotti puton.*
   Blood-thirsty forever.
   They mercilessly suck oak trees' sap;
   The trees encircle and protect my house.

These chilly autumn days
Looking for warm cozy life
Stinkbugs sneak into the house,
For more babies they make nests in every comer.
You meet them on a bookshelf, in the cupboard
Even inside your bed.

5. Touch Scots stinkbug with one finger!
   The bug instantaneously emits foul odor.
   You, nice-looking man, are transformed
   Into an ugly duckling.
   Before you can crush the bug,
   She coolly flies out of the room.
   Now the most beautiful planet of the solar system,
   The earth, becomes an unbearable stinking hell.

6. Enough, too much!
   I want out————of the insect world.
   Sleeping bag, toothbrush . . .
   Putting everything into age-old rucksack
   Decisively I start for No-Bug Land.

7. Crossing over two heaps of debris,
   The leftover of an angry typhoon—
   I walk along village road.
   Under awakening blue sky of autumn
   I watch white heads of old farmers
   Harvesting in rice field.

8. There another stinkbug!
   With no wings, but tires, it buzzes along at fifty miles per hour.
   Who handles the metallic armor-clad bug?
   The most famous Samurai stinkbug—

To the lowest caste, to miserable pedestrians
He shouts, "Out of my way, out of my way!"
Leaving a fart of glorious civilization
Samurai stinkbug disappears.

9. Turn Scots stinkbug on her back if you like!
   She will die if she can't turn back over by herself.
   Turn over the Samurai stinkbug if you like.
   He will die if he is lucky.

10. About structure and mechanism,
    There is no waste with Scot's stinkbug.
    Like a god this species is created perfectly.
    But Samurai stinkbug made of fancy jokes—
    Too big for a coffin
    Too small for paradise.
    And bug asks for more highways, more stench, more noise,
    More traffic tragedies, more Safety Traffic Weeks,
                                        more oil combinate
    More atomic energy, more nuclear weapons, more world war and
    More . . .

11. Standing on trembling suspension bridge
    Over quick-running, stinking river of desire
    I listen to rumbling echo of hell
    We are all going to.

12. Enough, too much!
    End of journey—I return home.
    Under kerosene lamp, upon a writing desk
    Here, another stinkbug
    Calmly breathing, meditating, and rambling.

OCTOBER 1982 *Shinano, Japan*

# An Abandoned Farmhouse

sky blue
mountain high
forest large
gorge deep
plenty of water.

water invites man here.
man draws water
 builds a shelter
 erects tombstones
 picks up bracken ferns
 gathers *Boletus edulis.*

he also sows adonis seeds
and waits for springtime.

today's winter solstice.
still no snow.

three persimmon trees
with many sweet fruits.
many chickadees.

huge piles of dung
underneath trees.

a black bear forgets his hibernation.

adonis buds break up frozen soil already.

for ten years

no man here.

# Specification for Mr. Nanao Sakaki 's House

I want to build my own house on our planet earth.
Today's January first, my sixtieth birthday.
Even now they call me a freak.
Even now I haven't my own house;
What a shame after many years of vagabond life—
Today I seriously decide to build my own house.

Where would my house stand?
The high Andes where glacier & desert meet,
Or Tropic of Cancer where coral reef & rain forest meet,
Or the taiga where the aurora protects the North Pole,
Or an island in East China Sea where great cedars raise
                                                young typhoons,
Or northern Yaponesia where beech trees make magnificent shade
                                                for wild beings,

Or a peninsula in the sea of Okhotsk where god blazes in
                                                volcanic crater.

Round-based conical house like a bird nest—
For example, American Indian tipi or Mongolian yurt;
Both buildings have no trouble with earthquake & typhoon.
Materials for construction should be plentiful & easily available.
For example—bamboo, cedar, clay, coral limestone, andesite.
For the cement—sweat, wisdom & friendship.

A microcosm—
Height 100M, radius 100M.
Bamboo & cedar for framework,

Lava & clay as basement
Blue columbine carpet,
Bougainvillea ceiling.
Pampas grass roofing;
Alive, breathing statues as wall—winter wren, golden eagle,
Sea plankton, sperm whale, dinosaur, salamander,
Myself, the representative of terrestrial mammals
Standing in a corner as keyboard;
      Me, & all the creatures in unison
      Pulsating heart rhythm
      Swirling breath melody—a life-roving song—
      The whole dome sounds bamboo pipe organ.

In night, without electricity
Light & mind play & build up a planetarium
To your eyes I call up not only all stars in heaven
But also 10,000,000,000 light year's future of the universe.

In the whole house, air-conditioning, water systems,
Every kind of food available all the time.
Still if you feel cold, hug somebody!
Still if you feel hot, be stark naked to the bones!
Still if you feel hungry, eat yourselves "full of beans"!
Still if you feel sad, gulp down hot soup of your tears!

This house is built for my lovely kids first.
And for everybody who wants to stay with me.
With a shovel I dig the frozen soil,
Where the stars, sun, wind & water celebrate.

Deep blue of mid-winter sky;
Here drop two, three, four snow flakes.
Far & dim I catch a whispering song—

Inviting, tempting song of Calypso the sea nymph.
My heart starts burning for an unknown land.
Throwing away the muddy shovel
Leaving snow-covered new house behind
I start for the unknown land.

# The Battle of Toads

*For Allen Ginsberg*


      Que-que-flash-bang!
      Me, a toad, going to the battlefield.
      Que-que-flash-bang!
Many years ago, so young, so confused
I was lost in the woods.
Under the evening sun in springtime,
What a surprise—along a mountain trail
I found a hundred toads walking with me.
      Que-que-flash-bang!

So ignorant, simply astonished and threatened,
No way to run away, no spot to stand still,
Just like a toad I walked with them.
      Que-que-flash-bang!

Quite suddenly not a single toad with me—
But dark and freezing night followed my steps.

Many years passed—these days I live in the woods.
One April day, after snow melted into lowland swamps
I found quite a long string made of transparent gelatin
With a thousand small black spots in it—
Toad eggs—outcome of toad battle.

Violets, Scotch broom, black locust—flowery May.
Each time you pass by these swamps
You squat down, open your eyes, your mind
And smile to watch tiny lively tadpoles.

High in the woods
Oriental cuckoo sings tender note to the earth—
Deep in the gorge
Deer frog pitches her song to heaven.


Massacre————one day, a pickup truck broke into an
                                    enchanted garden.


Tadpoles of toad, bullfrog, and salamander
Together with flowers of thistle and clover
All crushed down, rooted up or buried deep in the mud.
Massacre————in a few moments with a truck, eternal with
                                    living things.


Broken-hearted, I stand motionless
————Look, here again starts a parade of toads!
            Que-que-flash-bang!
            Me, a toad, going to the battlefield.
            Que-que-flash-bang!


In the parade, a man made of mud
Carries a truck on his back,
            Que-que-flash-bang!
Next comes the president of truck factory
Shouting, "You young Japanese should learn
How to drive the amphibian tanks"
And himself goes on a tank with a Japanese sun flag,
            Que-que-flash-bang!
After him, the paragons of once advanced nations:
Adolf Hitler, Harry S. Truman, Joseph V. Stalin;
Now holding nuclear warheads on their chests as glorious medals,
            Que-que-flash-bang!

Then, the great leaders of nuclear, electric industry of the world,
Just like holy men, all naked in full radioactive ash,
        Que-que-flash-bang!
After them, rather shady scientists, tricky journalists,
Intellectuals and a huge number of middle-class opportunists
All hand in hand, with a smile walk in the ruin of Word War III.
        Que-que-flash-bang!

More coming————
John with a compost bag, Peter a broad ax,
Nancy a loom. Bob a guitar and hoe,
Chris a fishing spear and a drum. . . . .and last of the parade,
Nanao with a homemade tofu-bomb,
        Que-que-Wake-Up!
        Me, a toad going to the battlefield.
        Que-que-flash-bang!

        High in the woods
        Oriental cuckoo sings tender note to the earth:
        Deep in the gorge
        Deer frog pitches her song to heaven.
                Rainy season starts today.

Deer frog, *Rhacophorus buergeri*

# Homo Erectus Ambulant

One more bouquet
For the tiny, watery, green star, the planet earth
—Homo erectus ambulant.


No two the same voice
No two the same eye
No two the same destiny
But with only one heart we human beings are born.


But as many voices of human beings
As many eyes
As many destinies,
Why so crazily varicolored, our human minds?


The end of August, 1983;
Three top articles in today's Tokyo newspaper:
    To Japanese politicos
    Huge donations from big corporations.
        At teachers' unions' gathering somewhere in western Japan
        Incredible violence by right wing.
    Tomorrow, Sept. 1st—60th anniversary of 1923 Tokyo earthquake,
    Magnitude 7.9. The dead 99,331. Missing 43,476.


Clouds and wind are drifting together in blue sky
On the watery and green earth
Spiderwort, pampas grass and camomile—
Flowers and seasons are rotating together round earth's axis.

Me, *Homo erectus* ambulant,
On the way home from a big town,
Heavy pack on my back.
Casually I halt my steps—
A cloud of horseflies are tempted by my sweaty skin . . .

In front of me, one meter, a viper winding her way . . .
In front of me, two meters, two Spanish flies hopping . . .
In front of me, five meters, a dragonfly and a swallowtail crossing
each other . . .

In front of me, ten meters, three crows flying off.

More than the number of all living creatures on earth—
Why so crazily varicolored our human minds?

*Homo erectus* ambulant—
One more bouquet for the planet earth.

Tomorrow's wind could be
North, south, east or west.

# Go with Muddy Feet

When you hear dirty story
          wash your ears.
When you see ugly stuff
          wash your eyes.
When you get bad thoughts
          wash your mind.
              and
Keep your feet muddy.

# Medical Certificate

Your legs become weak first.
Then your stomach, head.
Finally your mind becomes weak.

No, our mind becomes weak first.
Then your head, stomach.
Finally your legs become weak.

Not legs, nor mind—you,
Yourself become weak first.

# Bellybutton

The plants
Given life by minerals
Then give life to animals.

An animal called . . .
A man, you,
Stand with legs, eyes, nose & nipples.

A puppet, you
who work so hard
with two hands & a head.

When your navel starts laughing,
you are a song.

# November Song

In a November night
Under the kerosene lamp light
Around the clear flame of oaks in the open fire pit
We chatter and peel persimmons.
Tomorrow we will hang the naked fruits
Under the eaves for drying by sun, wind and frost.
    —Something running through darkness,
      Is that gushing wind or shower?

        . . . . .

The past is now.
Three hundred years ago
A Japanese potter named Kakiemon or Persimmon Jack
Tried so hard to catch the jewel light
Of persimmon in November sun,
Forgot to eat, to sleep, to talk.
Three years later he was able to bring out
The gorgeous color in his ceramics.

        . . . . .

The past is now.
Five years ago
An eighty one year old Japanese lady
Jumped into a nearby river
And finished her life under the November sky.

    —Beyond the old lady's reach
      There hung hundreds of flaming persimmon fruit
      Backed by heavenly blue
      In the dazzling sunshine.

—With her family and her friends
Sitting around the open firepit in November nights
She chattered and peeled the fruits
All her life, for eighty one years.

—Now living by herself
She can make the dried fruits no more
She can present the sweet jewel to friends no more.
Missing the cheerful work
No pleasure to live off
No treasure to share
The old lady sank into the cold river.

. . . . .

Stormy November night.
Something running through darkness—
Is that gushing wind or shower?
Around the fire pit we chatter and peel the fruits.

To chickadees, black bears and men
The tree offers cool shade in summer
Bittersweet cakes in autumn.
Botanists call the tree
    "Diospyros Kaki"

    "The flame of God"
Very bitter in the beginning
Very sweet at the end.
Is this the food of life
Or the light of life?

# Nut Trail

Breezy hillside.
Halfway up clearing trail
I start picking up walnuts.

> Walnuts, chestnuts, wild grapes . . .
> Nut trail, mushroom trail . . .
> Animal trail, human trail . . .
> Finally the trail diffuses into blue heaven.

Grassy hilltop.
A Blooming flower in front of me.
Who and what are you?
No answer.

> Loudly I call the flower by my lover's name
> Caressing with finger tips
> I wish to give my hands to her.

Now she has hands, legs and smiling face,
And suddenly jumps over me,
Passes through a spider's web,
Comes down as walnut.

> Here, I got you.

# A Biography

Many things to be done.
Many more things
        left behind undone
Therefore nothing to do now.
Spring wind
        shifts over
        my vacant face.

# Gloves

*For Allen, sixty light-years old glove.*


February midnight.
Cloud covered sky. Zero degrees centigrade.
Blew out the kerosene lamp
I watch the flame of burning oaks in the fireplace.
No moon, no stars, no snow
No wind, no friends to chatter with.
Only the murmur of a brook.

Wondering eyes of mine are captured
By four pairs of gloves
Which are drying and warming themselves around the fireplace.
Two cotton-pairs. Two leather-pairs.

Oh, my dear gloves, my brothers!
Unusually warm winter—little snow, thin ice.
Still it's not so easy
To dig out snow-buried firewood without your help.

Supple cotton gloves, you come from
The showy, flowery bolls of a plant.
Tough leather gloves, you come from
The skin of cow who eats plants and gives us milk.

But someday, you, the gloves will be broken down
To miserable rags.
And together with exhausted Hong Kong flowers

Together with exhausted plastic dolls
One day you will be burnt to ashes.

Me a glove—supple and tough one.
To protect somebody's fingers from frostbite,
If possible, to relieve somebody of his suffering by my hands
At least, to be in good shape for the tomorrow,
Clad in the human skin for the time being,
Squatting at the fireplace with four pairs of gloves
Watching the flame of burning oaks,
I make my body dry and warm.

As your pillows for the night,
Oh, my dear gloves, my brothers—
A smile's blooming on my cheeks.
Sleep well!

# Travel    Light

Pleasing smell of Sea urchins and sweet potatoes
Around the burning driftwoods.
Stormy night of spring.

In East China sea
On the beach of a tiny island
I find myself
Sitting in a cave
With a hundred human skulls
Who died by the smallpox
Three hundred years ago.

One by one
I listen to their stories
All night long.

As the rosy Dawn streaks
One of them mumbles

"To travel light
Why don't you leave your skull here?"

# Blue   Open   Sky

How lovely morning of June!

I send off three Kamikaze pilots
Who head for Okinawa
With a heavy bomb under the wing of
Training fighter, the Shiragiku or White chrysanthemum
At an air base in south Japan, 1945.

> One of them, Sgt. Goto looks like me
> With long hair and long beard.

Soon after taking off
They are besieged by Ten American fighters,
the Grumman hellcat.

Three silver winged coffins

Three dazzling fireballs

Three long-tailed question marks

In blue open sky.

# Come Come Rain

I listen to rain falling
    on a rotten thatched roof
I listen to rain falling
    on a full-blooming dogwood forest.
I listen to rain falling
    on a slanting planet earth.
I listen to rain falling
    on the far-sailing Halley's comet.

                    I listen to the rain falling
                    on Auschwitz, 1944,
                    on Hiroshima, 1945,
                    on Minamata, 1956.

I listen to rain falling
    on the last California condor.
I listen to rain falling
    on the last desert dream of Georgia O'Keeffe.
    who died in the spring, along with the condor
I listen to rain falling
    on Big Mountain, the land of Native Americans
I listen to rain falling
    on a coral reef, of Ishigaki, Okinawa.

By the old castle of Matsumoto, Japan,
I listen to rain falling on a congressman's election speech.
I listen to rain falling on bankers' suits
In the business center of Tokyo

I listen to rain falling on the land
of agri-chemical flowers full-blooming, in twentieth-century Japan.
I listen to rain falling on the TV show
of marvelous twenty-first-century world.

   In the rain
there runs a thunder's laughter.

      Come, come rain!

# Soil for Legs

Soil for legs
Ax for hands
Flower for eyes
Bird for ears
Mushroom for nose
Smile for mouth
Songs for lungs
Sweat for skin
Wind for mind
Just enough

# Manifesto

Hokkaido island will be an independent country.
Because the sea of Okhotsk, the mother ocean
dyes your heart pure indigo.
Because the primeval forest of Shiretoko peninsula
dyes your heart pure green.
Because the snow-covered Sarobetsu wasteland
dyes your heart pure white.

Hokkaido island will be an independent country.
Because yeddo spruces soar in clouds.
Because giant angelica flowers flame up in summer.
Because there are countless edible plants and mushrooms.

Hokkaido island will be an independent country.
Because you could see irreplaceable wild beings—
       grizzly bears, Blakiston's fish owls,
              black woodpeckers and Parnassus butterflies.

Hokkaido island will be an independent country
Because you can meet wonderful human animals—
       fishermen, farmers, mountain men, hobos,
          musicians, artists and poets.

Hokkaido island will be an independent country.
Because you can love delightful birds—
kids, women and men.

          This island is made as a garland
          No nuclear power plants

No agri-chemicals
No big corporations
No authorities
No arms.
We call this island Moshiri, the Peaceful Land—
                    after the Ainu's name

Now together with
Alaska, Tierra del Fuego, New Guinea, Yunnan and Siberia
let's start a Pacific Basin union.

And together with
Andromeda nebula, Orion constellation and
                    Magellanic clouds
let's start a Federation
          for the Universe.

# Ancestor of Japanese

September night.   Almost full moon.
In a clean kitchen, certainly no cockroach—
A drunkard, all naked except necktie, shouts,
        "Our ancestor is the Ainu."

No, absolutely not!
Neither Ainu nor American
but cockroach is the real ancestor of Japanese.

Here in Hokkaido, part of prosperous Japan
There is a community which wants to eat
The garbage of nuclear power plants
        "for better homes and gardens."

There are government officials
who want to cut down everybody's woods
called National Forests.
Living in a flower garden of fossil fuel and plastics
they import from Korea thirty-three million dollars a year
of Matsutake mushrooms as a delicacy.

And from China they buy
ten million Mamushi vipers as an aphrodisiac.
There are now one hundred million middle class
cockroaches in Japan they say.

The Japanese cockroach is also gulping down
the Amazonian rain forest for toilet paper.

For future generations,
they work vigorously and joyously
leaving the soil full of agri-chemicals,
leaving rivers and lakes terribly polluted
leaving graveyards of coral reefs.

In honor of the glorious Constitution of Japan
"toward the happy and cultural life"
they ask for more Koalas and missiles

In an old forest of yeddo spruce
                    a grizzly bear watches the full moon.

SEPTEMBER 1986                                    127

# Persimmon Vinegar

Pearly blue autumn sky.
Dry wind from Mongolia.

Late afternoon
We pick persimmons in our friend's garden.
Children laughing, shouting.

When the hills change into bright red
Gather the fruit
Cut off the bottom ends with knife
Clean the skins with water
Put them into a ceramic jar
Cover the top with a light wooden board
Keep the jar in a warm corner in your house.

Around May Day Festival
     —Strong smell from the jar!
It's already fermented.
Strain the juice through cotton gauze.
Here comes pearly liquid—pure natural vinegar.
Taste it, enjoy it, share it.

The flying goblin Tengu's favorite dish
     Young persimmon leaf,
          Rich in vitamin C
          Good for tempura
          Good for herb tea.

Dried in the sun and chilly autumn wind
The bitter fruit changes into sweet cake,
> Good for tea ceremony
> Good for your healthy life.

> Late in the night
> We relish ginger
> Pickled in persimmon vinegar,
> Sip Awamori, the rice spirit from Okinawa,
> Sing songs with drum and guitar,
> Slowly go deep into the jar of sleep
> To be ripened as the vinegar for tomorrow.

In the next life
We will be a persimmon forest.

# Let's Play Together Tomorrow

In a beautiful time
There was a shallow sea
With bountiful fish, shells, coral reef and dragon palaces.

Then the sea retreated
And Sugar Loaf was left to rise up on the plain.

Man came to the island and lived in peace quite long.

One day darkness came to the island
With two monstrous armies from north and east
And a crazy war started.

      Thousands of people were killed.
      Thousands of people were wounded.
      Thousands of people became insane.

Finally the war ended
And forty-one years passed like a wind.

Today there are still jet fighters in the sky.
Battle ships in the sea, military tanks on the hills.
How long must we live in such a narrow chasm of war?

      Chilly autumn wind.
      Far away shiny ocean waves, and setting sun.

Here on Sugar Loaf
Where once tremendous blood and tears ran down in the war

Now stand side by side
A Buddhist temple and a Catholic church.

Chilly autumn wind.
Far away shiny ocean waves, and setting sun.

When I walk down the hill
Where Shakyamuni and Jesus Christ stand side by side
Two little boys shout to me.

"Going home now?"
"Yes."
"Let's play together tomorrow!"

Here on Sugar Loaf
Where once tremendous blood and tears ran down in the war
Little Shakyamuni and little Jesus Christ shout,

"let's play together tomorrow!"

*Sugar Loaf is a hill situated in the northeast part of Naha, Okinawa, fifty meters above sea level. At the end of WWII the battle fought there cost 2662 American Marine lives, and left 1289 insane.*

NOVEMBER 1986

# Rowing in the Snow Ocean

With icicles on my beard
Snowshoes and ski poles
I row in the snow ocean.

With binoculars around my neck
A warm teapot in a daypack
And a raccoon's hide on my buttocks
I row in the snow ocean.

Once upon a time
there were two earths:  A and B.
While Earth A stayed in the solar system,
Earth B, one day, flew to the other side of the Milky Way.

Earth A is right now a megaslum of several billion robots,
Earth A blushes with shame whenever a rainbow appears
because her original beauties, the green mountains
                              and blue waters are gone forever.

I'm told Earth B is abundant in splendid flowers,
birds and animals.
And the people there wear rainbow robes
                              and chatter with dance and song.

January 1986.
At the Sierra foothill of North America on Earth A
here black oak and black-tailed deer are prosperous
I sent a letter through Halley's comet
To the post office on Earth B
Asking for my immigration visa.

One year passed.
Today at the Taisetsu foothill of Yaponesia on Earth A
Where the hills are occupied by tree farms fir and larch
And a few humble stands of oak and willow are left as remnants,
where the eyes of tit, jay and nuthatch hold
the vanishing flame of life, where the footprints of fox,
             hare and squirrel give us a hint of man's tomorrow
I row in the snow ocean waiting for Earth B's answer.

In the afternoon, sepia clouds over the western horizon.
Deep blue heaven over the eastern silver-gray peaks.
Flurry after flurry.

On a hilltop I check the direction of Earth B with a compass
And am ready to send up a shout—
        POST OFFICE ON EARTH B, PLEASE!
        POST OFFICE ON EARTH B, PLEASE!
        THIS IS NANAO ON EARTH A CALLING!

To my throbbing heart Here
flies back Earth B's message—

    COME BACK ANYTIME!

So far to Earth B.
I wish to hitch on Halley's comet halfway.

        Waiting for the comet in the year 2062
        With icicles on my beard
        Snowshoes and ski poles
        I row in the snow ocean.

# SOUTH POLE STAR

# Oct. 1, 1981

Suddenly you stop walking.

With rainbow-edged Cero-cumulus drop clouds
The sun's corona brightens desert.

Ten days after the spring equinox.
Almost tropic of Capricorn.
25 degrees south, 131 degrees east.
The center of a continent.

Hot dry, westerly wind.
Without flapping,
Three huge eagles—the wedge tails,
Gliding in blue heaven.

Over a gigantic red monolith,
sheer and high,
The birds disappeared.

You begin walking again.

—Even eagle can fly, Why don't you?—

# Platypus

I want to see you, platypus, in the wild.
    Living in a burrow,
    Duck's bill, turtle's egg, mammalian milk.

I've been in Australia over a month already.
    Sinus, Canopus, Achemar,
    Centaurus Alpha & Beta,
    Southern cross, Magellanic clouds.

    Acacia, Eucalyptus, Spinifix, Mangrove.
    Black Swan, Bustard Turkey
    Kookaburra, Galah, Bell Bird.

    Goanna, Echidna, Kangaroo alive or dead,
    Dingo, Homo-sapiens black or white.

I want to see you platypus in the wild.
    Living in a burrow,
    Duck's bill, turtle's egg, mammalian milk.
    You never show me your face.

Australia, you platypus!
    Living in a burrow
    Duck's bill, turtle's egg, mammalian milk.
    You never show me your face.

Australia, you platypus!
>
> I'm tired of your tricks.
> Living in a burrow
> Duck's bill, turtle's egg, mammalian milk.

Australia, you platypus!
>
> Don't hesitate
> To show your noble spirit.

Australia,
>
> I want to see you in the wild.

# Chant of a Rock

So long, so long————
Forty thousand years
I wait for you.

At last
After forty thousand years
You come back to me.

These days
They call me a giant monolith of Tierra del Australia.
No, I'm neither rock nor cave.

    Look at my skin, touch my skin!
    Why is it so shiny?
    Ah, black diamond!
    Brighter than the Milky Way.
    Why is it so polished, so refined?

    Me————
    Tended, caressed, loved
    By your fingers
    By your eyes
    By your heart
    By your songs
    Forty thousand years.

    Look at my skin, touch my skin!
    Shiny————warm————tough.
    Full of light

Full of strength
Full of love.

Touch me tenderly with your fingers
As your gran'pa did yesterday.

Kiss me softly with your lips
As your gran'ma did last year.

Sleep by me in peace
As you did forty thousand years ago.

Australia————a wonderful dreamland forever.
Now they call me a treasure of Commonwealth of Australia.

Ladies and gentlemen,
Welcome to the dreamland!
Welcome to the magical rock!

Please enter air-conditioned Australia.
Please enjoy air-conditioned Australia.

But, ladies and gentlemen,
Don't forget what happened here in the dreamtime.

Remember Wounded Knee in Australia
Remember Auschwitz in Australia
Remember Hiroshima in Australia
Remember a shiny rock in the dreamland!

So long, so long—
Forty thousand years
I wait for you

OCTOBER 1981 *Started in Central Australia*
DECEMBER 1981 *Finished at Zuni Village, North America*

# Break the Mirror

In the morning
After taking cold shower
————what a mistake————
I look at the mirror.

There, a funny guy,
Gray hair, white beard, wrinkled skin,
————What a pity————
Poor, dirty, old man!
He is not me, absolutely not.

Land and life
Fishing in the ocean
Sleeping in the desert with stars
Building a shelter in mountains
Farming the ancient way
Singing with coyotes
Singing against nuclear war—
I'll never be tired of life.
Now I'm seventeen years old,
Very charming young man.

I sit down quietly in lotus position,
Meditating, meditating for nothing.
Suddenly a voice comes to me:

> "To stay young,
> To save the world,
> Break the mirror."

# Little Captain Cook/Penguin

Moonless night,
Stars, sea breeze, white breakers, cool sand.
Wafting smell of dead and life.

From the equator
Forty-four degrees south.
Crossing another stretch of waters
You will reach Antarctica.

On the southern shore of Tasmania,
Standing motionlessly in dusk
I wait for
The landing of Captain Cook.

Behind a long stretch of white sand
Many burrows are scattered in bushy hill.
Who lives here?
Poseidon, dinosaur, bird or human being?

From the beach
Here comes a small creature!
35 cm tall
Waddling gait
All wet, slick feathers
In a black and white tuxedo made in London
Long arms
A tiny computer on his left wrist
Yes, Little Captain Cook/Penguin.

Following him
Queen of England,
Mr. Industrial Revolution,
Napoleon and his million toy soldiers,
General Custer from Wounded Knee, North America,
Mr. First World War,
Adolf Hitler the Third Reich,
After him Mr. Second World War.

Last, here comes Mr. Third World War!
35 cm tall
Waddling gait
All wet, slick feathers
In a black and white tuxedo made in London
Long arms
A tiny computer on his left wrist.

Almost midnight.
Everybody sound asleep in their burrows.
But, Mr. Third World War finds
No burrow, no home, no supper for him.

In the waters
All day long
He eats and eats
A lot of fish and a lot of oil balls.
Still he is hungry and angry.
Now he starts fighting against himself.
Finally, Mr. Third World War eats up himself.

Wafting smell of dead and life.
Moonless night.

Stars, sea breeze, white breakers, cold sand.
Motionless I stand in dark
On the southern shore of Tasmania.

Where is Tasmanian Tiger?
Where is Tasmanian Aborigine?
Where is Homo sapien?

I look toward southern heaven.

Half way to zenith
There, a brilliant star!
Impossible————South Pole Star!

Stars, sea breeze, white breakers, cool.
Wafting smell of dead and life.
Moonless night.


*Little Penguin, Eudyptula minor.*

# DESERT RAT

# Far Above the Grand Canyon

Hot, very hot afternoon—
Far above the Grand Canyon
A gigantic cloud—
Just like the Grand Canyon.
I start walking on the cloud
The cloud slowly sails back to the ground.

Cutting through the bottom of heaven—
Muddy, swift shaft of waters
                              —The Colorado.

I keep walking—
Hot, very hot sand trail without end.

# Small People

"inch by inch
little snail,
creep up and up Mt. Fuji."
—Issa, 19th century Haiku poet.

. . . "a Navaho woman identifies
801 specimens of desert insects."
an American scientist recorded—1948.

3,000,000 abandoned children
in big Brazilian cities.

3,000,000 soldiers
in Red China.

a Pennsylvanian sea lily fossil
300,000,000 years old
from the Santa Fe basin,
now paperweight on my desk.

I want to be a lightning bug
for the coming 300,000,000
light years' dark age.

# Happy New Year!

Happy New Year!
Happy Birthday!

In the afternoon
Dec. 31st, 1981,
To celebrate New Year
And my 59th birthday, Jan. 1st,
I clean a window glass with vinegar.

Why "Happy New Year"?
Because I clean a window glass.

As a grammar school kid
I cleaned the windows of classrooms.
As a teenage worker
I cleaned the office windows.
As a soldier
During wartime
I cleaned the windows of barracks.
After the war
I cleaned many windows of offices, factories and houses.
Today—
To celebrate New Year
And my 59th birthday
I clean a window glass with vinegar.

All our lifetime
Even after your death
You clean windows with vinegar.

The world needs window cleaners.
Hi, Nanao,
The world needs you!

Through the window
Through leafless Gambel oaks
Through freezing, pure, transparent air
I catch a glimpse of a large hawk.

"Rough-legged Hawk"—I'm sure,
Winter visitor from Alaska.

Hi, Rough-legged Hawk!
You, tireless, fearless flier!
You know nothing about your birth
You know nothing about your death.
You just soar, glide, hover,
And also
You are a window cleaner.
With each flapping
You clean the winter sky.

In your wake
No dust
No junk.
You just leave
Clear, sweet, profound blue sky for everybody.

The world needs window cleaners.
Hi, rough-legged Hawk,
The world needs you!

Happy New Year!
Happy Birthday!

# Valentine's Day

You have no touch of class,
         no touch of uniqueness,
         no touch of elegance,
         no touch of mystery . . .

    I love you!

# A Big Day

Getting water at the spring

Carrying firewood

Chattering with a neighbor

The sun goes down.

A big day.

# Top Ten of World Music

Australian Aborigines' Music

Gamelan Orchestra of Indonesia

Raga from India

Nomad song of Niger, West Africa

Andean Flute Music

Jamaican Reggae

Navaho's night chant, North America

Japanese Shakuhachi Music

Tibetan Buddhist chanting

Your own music.

# Who Am I?

I'm poet because they call me so.

Psychiatrist, because
            everybody in the world is insane.
Ecology freak, because I'm Mr. Nature.
Free in love, free in spirit.
Without reason, crazy for music.
Cook dinner for everybody.
Friend of anyone who walks with me.
I'm a Third Stone Age Man.

            A week ago————
            In Chihuahua desert. North America,
            At the Continental Divide
            Smiled to see a flaming Indian Paintbrush
            And ate venison and black Bear meat.

            Today————
            Back home to northern mountain
            Under evening moonlight
            I sing and weep for love with robins.

MARCH 31, 1982

# In and Out

Your soul is Buddha————
Your body, temple.
Your mountain, enlightened.

Last night
Under Gegenschein
Under sun's counterglow toward Zodiac
I sang with coyotes.

Breakfast in the late morning:
Tempeh with baby dandelions,
Organic cow liver with dark green nettle leaves,
Cup of jasmine tea.

About noon
I wrote many letters to friends.

Stand up to Nuclear War!
To protect Universal Citizenship of All Living Things,
To have all our life and death in peace,
Stand up to Nuclear War!

In the afternoon,
In the meadow near by,
A turkey vulture,
The first one in spring,
Drops her shit on my hat.

APRIL 1982 *El Salto Peak, N.M.*

# Indian Summer

A robin's love call
On a pine tree top

        Indian Summer

Today
Somewhere
Somebody
Makes a nuclear bomb
Just to kill you

        Indian Summer

Three
Tiny
Yellow flowers of
Dandelion

# Fifth Deer

A song—far away.

A man?
A coyote?
Or Halley's comet?

For hours
Empty handed
Absent minded
I sit alone
In a tiny shack
In a black oak forest.

Above the overcast
Somewhere
The moon shadows
Where is the dawn now?

There, wandering—over the fallen oak leaves
Black-tailed deer.
One, two, three, four.

As the fifth deer
I follow them.

Somewhere
Right now
—I'm sure—
The world sleeps very well.

# North America

At Superstition mountain in the Sonora desert
A beer-bellied man is shooting
At a fifty foot Saguaro cactus with a rifle.
A couple of minutes later the giant cactus falls to the ground
and kills the man—April 1984.

April 1986
In a ravine at Big mountain in Hopi and Navajo land
A coyote is reading "The Wall Street Journal."
——How many mice can I steal next year
From the American economy?

Off the coast of northern California
Sea lions are listening
to the long-term weather forecast on the radio
——They want to freeze-dry the redwood forest
For the coming ice age.

On a rocky ledge
Somewhere in the century of nuclear power
A family of California condors is watching
"Wild Kingdom" on TV.
——They ponder how many more years
    Homo sapiens, one of the most endangered species
    can survive?

# LET'S EAT STARS

# Song of Lichen

*To my sister Iku*

In the village graveyard
a seven-year-old boy cries silently
"Why, why?"
at his sister's burial.

His eighteen-year-old sister
who taught him Lady Murasaki's poetry
who knitted him an orange wool sweater
whose soft black hair hung to her waist
is going underground.

During a thunderstorm on a summer evening
this sister, sobbing,
held him tightly in the bath tub.

Now she goes to terra incognita.
The boy cries silently,
"Why, why?"

As a provisional answer
they build a small tombstone for her
and lichen grows over
very slowly.

One lovely morning
the boy becomes a tombstone

and lichen grows over
very slowly.

Tomorrow you
Still hear the song of the lichen:
"Why, why?"

# Fireflies

*For the painter Akira Goto, who hanged*
*himself on the Nichinan coast of Japan*


A call far away—
In between beach and woods.

Yes, I hear you, Akira!
Your breathing liberates crawling caterpillars.
Your eardrums vibrate wind strings.
Your heart always strides on wave ridges.

Akira!
With nodding or smiling
you changed yourself into a tiny wild rose.
With sudden silence you now ring a chime on the ocean.

Akira!
This is the season of blossoms.
Under the mimosa which
gently took your dead body
I stand in rain.
I stand in vain.

Akira!
The rain stops suddenly.
On the cliff facing the ocean
where once you stood with me
where once the evening glow shone in your eyes
two fireflies fade into dark night.


JUNE 1968

# Miracle

Air, wind, water, the sun
      all miracle.

The song of Red-winged Blackbird
      miracle.

Flower of Blue Columbine
      miracle.

Come from nowhere
Going nowhere,
       miracle.

# Oh My Buddha

Cherry blossoms, geisha girls and computer country
—Japan produces thirty percent other staple food
and imports as much grain as all Africa needs.

Ninety percent of Japanese believe they are middle class.

Five river otters survive on Shikoku's rocky shore,
runaways from contaminated rivers.
—to exterminate the rest
Tokyo government already concreted
more than half of Japan's sea coast.

With the help of a starfish, the crown of thorns,
Japan destroyed ninety percent other coral.
Here, another Kamikaze project
—last motherly reef of Okinawa
maybe soon buried
underneath a new tourist airport

> In World War II
> America never bombed
> Nara nor Kyoto
> in reverence for
> their temples, gardens, and spirit.

Today an ancient shrine in Nara
wants to cut down its sacred grove
for a tourist parking lot.

Kyoto is now "protected"
by thirteen nuclear power plants
within a radius of one hundred miles.

Tokyo awaits
not only an earthquake
and the eruption of Mt. Fuji
but also the fallout from a nuclear power plant
one hundred miles north.

To celebrate a holy and beautiful volcano
the U. S. Navy will build an airfield
in the national park of Miyake Island
one hundred miles south of Tokyo.

        Hot news
        from Halley's Comet!

        By the demand of all
        American citizens
        the Japanese Air Force
        has started building
        a Kamikaze Air Base
        in the heart of Yosemite National Park

# Daylight Moon

Only
life
can
give
you
life.

A young
cottontail
skips
over
the
snow.

Daylight Moon.

# Who Needs Allen Ginsberg in Today's Japan?

Air
Water
Soil
Coral reefs
Oak virgin forests
Ezo grizzlies
River otters
Iriomote wildcats
Ainus
Okinawans
Korean-Japanese
Happy middle class
Unhappy millionaires
Gays
Lesbians
Beggars
Criminals
Hobos
Organic farmers
Fishermen
No Nukes
Free Schools
Children
Housewives
Musicians
Artists
Poets
Leaves of grass
Roots

FEBRUARY 1988 *East Village, NYC*

# Boys, Be Ambitious!

Tierra del Fuego . . .
South Pole . . .
Mt. Everest . . .
The Moon . . .
Mars . . .
Sirius . . .
Seventh Heaven . . .
What's next?

> "Boys,
> Clean the kitchen first,
> Please!"

# Always

man with woman always
woman with flower
flower with bird
bird with wind
wind with cloud
cloud with sky
sky with you always.

# Let's Eat Stars

Believe me, children!

God made
Sky for airplanes
Coral reefs for tourists
Farms for agrichemicals
Rivers for dams
Forests for golf courses
Mountains for ski resorts
Wild animals for zoos
Trucks and cars for traffic tragedies
Nuclear power plants for ghost dance.

Don't worry, children!
The well never dries up.

Look at the evening glow!
Sunflowers in the garden.
Red dragonflies in the air.

A small child starts singing:

> "Let's eat stars!"
> "Let's eat stars!"

September 1988 *Mt. Taisetsu, Japan*

# Prague

*(Prologue for Nanao's book of poems,* Earth B, *published in Czech)*

Once upon a time
I was a glass cutter in Prague.
That time
They called me Rainer Maria Rilke.

Once upon a time
I was a violinist in Prague.
That time
They called me Franz Kafka.

Once upon a time
I was flower gardener in Prague.
That time
They called me Karel Capek.

Once upon a time
I was a brewer in Prague.
That time
They called me Nanao Sakaki.

SEPTEMBER 1988 *Mt. Taisetsu, Japan*

# Bikki Salmon

Bikki salmon swimming
Nanao salmon swimming
Allen salmon swimming
Gary salmon swimming
Black Elk salmon swimming
Issa salmon swimming
Lao Tsu salmon swimming
Ezo wolf salmon swimming
Ainu Koroppocl salmon swimming
Yamanba witch salmon swimming
Maitreya Buddha salmon swimming
Northern Cross salmon swimming.

Fair-weather cumulus floating
In October morning sky.
Rosy fruits of mountain ash trembling.
I stand on the cemented bank
of the River Teshio, Hokkaido, Japan.
A river straightened and strangled by man,
And on the bank, scattered eggs of salmon
Left by a poacher.

Orion high in the evening sly
Geese and swans head southward
Maple leaves burning red
Deer cry for love in a fir forest
Boletus edulis and wild grape invite you into mountains

*(Koroppocl—mythological Ainu goblin)*

Just before the sea of Okhotsk
Begins to shine with drifting ice
North Pacific salmon return to mother rivers
Where woods and waters nursed them years before.

Salmon means
Blood and meat to grizzly
Fish of God to Ainu
Fish of festival to Japanese.

In the pebbly river
Against quick running water
Holding their energy
They wait and wait
And suddenly, thrusting their fins
They leap up the stream
—Hurry to the spot of their birth and death.

Following holy belt of destiny
Tracing water thread of mystery
Today they lay eggs
Today they die here.

Bikki Sunazawa, legendary Ainu artist
For him too the time has come.
While cutting a woodblock print of the fish of God
He becomes a salmon.
Having fish eyes, nose, scales, tattoos
Spirals and soul
He's now a seventy-centimeter-long fish, Bikki salmon.

Pectoral fin, dorsal fin
Ventral fin, adipose fin, anal fin.

Under the river banks, heaps of trash
. . . TV sets, refrigerators
. . . chemical flotsam in the water
. . . acid rain and radiation in the air.

     Against the flow of poison
     Against the flow of decay
     Mumbling Heart Sutra
     Bikki salmon swimming.

In this crooked generation
Salmon moves straight forward.

Now the ripples ripple in unison:

     "Sing, dance as the river flows!
     Sing, dance as life flows!
     Sing, dance with your friends!"

Bikki salmon swimming
Nanao salmon swimming
Allen salmon swimming
Gary salmon swimming
Black Elk salmon swimming
Issa salmon swimming
Lao Tsu salmon swimming
Ezo wolf salmon swimming
Ainu Koroppocl salmon swimming
Yamanba witch salmon swimming
Maitreya Buddha salmon swimming
Northern Cross salmon swimming.
Bikki, Bikki
Bikki salmon swimming
In River Teshio.

# Red Fuji

Hi Hokusai—
Looking for your Mt. Fuji
I saunter about Izu peninsula.

In bushes
Hang pink seeds of woody bitter-sweet.

To the north
A mountain top . . . snow clad . . . Red Fuji
Rises above thick smog.

To the west
Blazing red sun setting into Suruga Bay.

Across the smoggy bay
A nuclear power plant.

On a wintry hill top . . .
Hi Hokusai!
What should I offer
To the last flower of gentian?

# Twilight Man

Before sunrise
I ramble along the Nagara River
In thick fog.

Among pebbles in the riverbed
One broken piece of earthenware
Neolithic Japan . . . perhaps five thousand years old.

In twilight fog
Somebody walking in front of me
Just a shadow.

Is he the earthenware maker?

Mingling with pebbles
Mingling with fog
Drifting on river
Drifting into history's debris
I will be a twilight man
Tomorrow.

What will be my earthenware?

# Great Purple

A big sign board in a railway station near Mt. Fuji:
"Welcome to the village of Great Purple."

"What is Great Purple?" I wonder.

The author of the *Tale of Genji*, Lady Murasaki?
A piece of purple sky floating in my lover's eyes?
A cloud made of purple wine passing over Mt. Fuji?
The color of a full-blooming magnolia's root?
The shadow of a star visible only to birds?
The light of the last water you drink?
or
Great Purple Butterfly?

Yes, it is!

Familia: NYMPHAUDAE
Genus: *Sasakia*
Species: *Charonda Hewitson*

Distribution: Eastern Asia
National Butterfly of Japan

# If I Have Tomorrow

Nov. 3rd, 1990
Pinacate desert, Mexico.
Celebrate the full moon
Overlooking Elegante Crater.

Jan. 1st., 1993—my 70th birthday.
With donkey, horse and camel
Start walking across Eurasia,
Korea to England.

Sometime in 1999
Organize the tribal gathering of "Earth B".

Jan. 1st, 2023—my 100th birthday
Climb the highest peak in the solar system
. . . Mt. Olympus, 25,000 meter volcano on Mars.

Jan. 1st, 2923—my 1000th birthday.
Visit "Miranda" . . . a moon of Uranus
For a rendezvous with Miss Miranda,
The fairy of Shakespeare's Tempest.

Jan. 1st, 11,923—my 10,000th birthday
Work hard for a new solar system
As a grain of stardust in the Milky Way.

OCTOBER, 5TH, 1990 *Santa Fe, S. Rockies*

# In Honor of the Persian Gulf War

Before robbery
There was ownership.

Before ownership
There were things.

Before things
There was nothing.

Before nothing
There was robbery.

FEBRUARY 1991 *Mt Taisetsu Japan*

# Song of Ashes Left on the Sand
# by a Gypsy Caravan

Spring has come.
One day Gypsy caravan stopped by Nagara River, Japan.

Along the Nutria rat's watercourse
With the wind over yellow mustard flowers,
Gypsy caravan stopped by Nagara River.

Common terns flashing
Their white wings in blue sky,
Young sweet fish flashing
Iridescent dorsal fins upon green water;
Gypsy caravan pitched tents
On the riverbed pebbles.

In the evening
They cooked brown rice on driftwood fire.

In the morning
Leaving ashes of songs and dances on the sand
They walk away to the terra incognita.

"Song of ashes"

Beyond the mountain range
Runs a river in a green forest,

*Nutria: Myocastor Coypus*
*90 cm. long. S. American water rat now wide spread in Japan*          183

Down the river ocean opens.
Beyond the ocean a land opens.

On the land a river runs in a green forest.
There, in the green forest
Unknown birds sing songs,
Unknown animals ramble
Deep in the blooming forest
Lives somebody in peace, they say.

Beyond the mountain range
Deep in the blooming forest
Lives somebody in peace.

Song of ashes left on the sand
    By Gypsy Caravan.

# Spring, Come Here!

Never again seventeen years old!
Never again the flowers of a dead tree!
                —14th century Japanese song.

As I kiss a magnolia flower
The vernal Goddess
Jumps into the mountain brook,
Floats away—

To up-stream
I climb, shouting

"Spring, come here!'
"Come to me!"

# Who Comes To Us

"Tau Tau Tarari Tara Lira!
Tau Tau Tarari Tara Lira!:
Humming an ancient tune of Japan
We ramble in snow mountains.

All of a sudden
Big, fat, ferocious-looking fellow!
B, B, B, BEAR!

Sepia-colored coat.
Weight: about 100 kg.
Sex: unidentified.
East-Asian Black Bear, Family *Ursidae*.

Feb 16th, 1992 Sunday. 3.00 PM.
Sky: cloudy, windy, snow flakes.
Temperature -2° C.
36°21'N. 138°25'E.
Chipuma Basin, central Japan.
Southern slope of Mt. Asama.
Right bank of Yanagizawa gorge.
Altitude 1350 meters
Mixed forest of oak, white birch, red pine.
Snow 30 cm.
Animal trails: fox, marten, rabbit, copper pheasant
Us: one female dog, one woman, two men.

When the big, fat, ferocious-looking fellow
Came up close, 20 meter

Our small dog "Koko"
Chased the bear down into the gorge.

"Tau Tau Tarari Tar -Lira!
Tau Tau Tarari Tara Lira!
Humming an andent tune of Japan
We ramble in a snow valley.
All of a sudden
An animal comes to us:

A raccoon dog
A dead one.

Dark-brown coat dappled with gold and silver,
No wound, no decayed tooth, no smell of death.
Beady eyes in blackish ninjya mask.
Male, full-grown.
Weight: about 8 kg.
Raccoon dog, Family *Canidae.*

He lies underneath the pampas grass roofed cave
Of reconstructed stone age cabin,
Not far from a twentieth century ruin:
Industrial-waste dumping ground.

Next morning
Chanting the Heart Sutra
We buried the raccoon dog
At the pampas-grass-land.

From his grave
Southeast by south
115km
Mt. Fuji.

# Kokopelli

"I'm a song
I walk here"—Ancient Hopi.

Here means
Where day break meets you.

Here means
Where a breeze meets you.

Here means
Where flowers meet you.

Here means
Where birds meet you.

Here means
Where a song meets you.

I'm a song
I walk here.

# Ear Means

Ear means

Where you listen to your own voice
Before your birth

Where your sleepy baby's fingers
Want to touch

Where your burnt finger tips
Quickly go to cool

Where your shyness blooms
In peach pink

Where goes the whisper
"I love you!"

Ten, twenty warblers chattering
In a morning wood of spring
I stand still with closed eyes.

In the water, beyond coral reef
Giving my ears and chest to humpback whale song.

Squall, thunderbolt, typhoon . . .
Look . . . there cloud's ear-lobe rising!

Saying farewell to the setting sun
I listen to high tide breakers
Coming from Milky Way horizon.

Ear means a shell sitting in the wind.

MAY 1992  *Bonin Island W. Pacific.*

# Somewhere on the Water Planet

In the beginning
There was a forest, a beech forest.
The forest gathered rain & divided rivers.
Rivers that nourished all breathing creatures.

Through long summer days
We, honorable descendants
Of *Yamanba* (mountain witch), *Kappa* (river goblin)
Walk down-river to the ocean.

On the path, scorching sun-beams
& sometimes torrential downpours.
In the bush, gnats, mosquitoes, ticks, newts & vipers.
At day's end, the darker the night, the brighter the moon & stars.

Our first meeting—*Megalobatrachns japonicus*
A giant salamander, who knows nothing
Of the extinction of dinosaurs or the end of the atomic age,
At ease in a pool by himself.

Next, a piece of Neolithic jar,
Shattered by a summer thunderbolt,
Buried deep in river-bank for five thousand years,
Waiting for some-one to pick it up.

In the blue sky, something dazzling drifting—
White porcelain, or fair weather cumulus?

Far away . . . typhoon;
Sound of a swallow skimming over a big dragon-fly
Resting on a trembling reed.

Ripples & children—the sun's dew drops—
Play in the same flow.
Diving, swimming, chattering together.

Cooking brown rice with driftwood on dry river-bed—
Dear sweet smell of campfire in years long-gone!
Dear living memories of forest life in Neolithic times.
Under a roaring tsunami of golf balls
Many time-honored beech forests are drowning today.

This is a flow—
Binding forest to ocean or yesterday to tomorrow.
Look—fisherman's arms, fishing-pole, fishing-line, fishing-hook!
There at the end of the line, brilliant silver light reflecting.
Is that a sweet-fish, or a bubble of toxic waste-water?

One day from the ocean, from yesterday, I'm sure
A lost hump-back whale will swim up this river.
And someday, from the ocean, from tomorrow,
Countless whales will swim up the river
To revisit the ancient beech forest,
Whales swimming up the river, up the river.

# Altitude 10,700M

Somewhere on the planet Earth
Somewhere on the western ridge of the Pacific volcanic rim
Altitude 10,700m, direction NNE, 850 kilometers per hour
Temperature inside 24°C, outside minus 50°C.

Through the tiny window of Pandora's box
As far as the eye can reach
Thousands of fine-weather cumulus sailing in the sky ocean
Far down below the clouds
Deep blue open water flower opening—the Philippine sea.

In vertical order:
Earth's crust, sea water, troposphere & stratosphere
Cutting through this canvas horizontally—
Monsoon & typhoon,
Coconut palm, mangrove, banyan tree & taro potato
Sperm whale, macaque monkey, flying fish & coral polyp,
Little tern, common cuckoo & barn swallow
Move north or south in between sky & ocean.

Do they keep to a timetable?
And who is that, carrying his old backpack?

Above the cumulus cloud ocean
Dark blue sky without end.
Draw on it any picture you want.

Like a white ball of kapok fruit
From your moldy pocket of hope

You pull out a funeral robe
Or butterfly wings which will open tomorrow.

Suddenly—an unexpected green island,
On the blue East China Sea. Yaku-shima?
No, too small,
And we are still farther south
Most likely Kita Daito, Okinawa.

Fair weather cumulus gone behind
Now ever-rising cumulo-nimbus mountains
One, two, three . . .
Much higher—colorful cirro-stratus dancing girls line up.

To know exactly where you are—
Captive in three-dimensional space—
When does the trap begin? Where does it end?

Congratulations!
Not only your own anxieties or adventures
But all the junk of the universe
Stuck in your backpack forever.

Georgia O'Keeffe died before she could tell me
About the map of Red China left by the Peking Man.

Neanderthal prophecy:
December 31st, 1999
Planet Earth will burst into flame
and go back to nothing.

Through the tiny window of descending Pandora's box
Japan rising up—
Poorly wooded hillsides, greenhouse farms, golf courses . . .
Kii peninsula? Yes.
Passing through heavy gray smog
Toward the invisible airport
Toward the invisible tomorrow
Jet engine thunders.

Soon landing . . .
Unsettled passengers.
Stewardess announces something in a high-pitched voice.

Yet the earth turns.

OCTOBER 30TH, 1992 *Nagoya Airport, Japan*

# Congratulations

In a tiny Tasmanian pond
Under the Gondwanan tree-ferns
Three platypuses come to see you,

                Congratulations!

Aboriginal Rainbow Serpent's dream comes true—
A marginal part of the Water Planet
Is glowing green today,

                Congratulations!

Near the ruin of a glacier cathedral
You weave a good dream tonight,

                Congratulations!

Someday, one of your grandchildren
Will meet a living dinosaur
Under the tree-fern right here,

                Congratulations!

Wind whispers—
"Homo sapiens can
Inhabit Pangaea, the super continent
A little longer,

                Congratulations!"

FEBRUARY 1993 *Mt. La Perouse, Tasmania*

# Dear Friend

Nothing happens
Without its end
Either good or bad.

Dear friend!
Don't worry—walk away
Don't walk—run!
Don't run—fly!
Don't fly—sleep well!
Dear friend!

# Autobiography

Born of a humble & poor family,
Received minimum education,
Learnt how to live by himself at fourteen,
Survived storms, one after another.
Bullets, starvation & concrete wastelands.

A day's fare—a cup of brown rice, vegetables,
Small fish, a little water, & a lot of wind.
Delighted by children & women,
Sharing beads of sweat with farmers,
Fishermen, carpenters & blacksmiths,
Paying no attention to soap, shampoo,
Toilet paper & newspapers.

Now & again
Loves to suck the nectar of honeysuckle,
To flutter with dragonflies & butterflies,
To chatter with winter wrens,
To sing songs with coyotes,
To swim with humpback whales,
And to hug rocks in which dinosaurs sleep.

Feels at home in Alaskan glaciers,
Mexican desert, virgin forests of Tasmania,
Valley of Danube, grasslands of Mongolia,
Volcanoes in Hokkaido & Okinawan coral reefs.

And—one sunny summer morning
He will disappear quietly on foot
Leaving no shadow behind.

# Wisdom

As the blooming cherry flowers
Withered away yesterday
Everything in the world
Fades away
Someday and forever.

And today again
You cross the mountains of living
Carrying false dreams
Quite seriously.

(from *Iroha*—ancient Japanese alphabetic song)

# Magic Pouch

On pilgrimage
to holy mountain Croagh Patrick
on Ireland's west coast
I found my magic pouch missing.

from Guatemala, some years ago
a black, white and purple cotton pouch
arrived and attached itself to my waist.

inside the pouch—
an Irish five pound note.
an army knife.
 a fountain pen.
 a magnifying glass.
a pair of sunglasses.

to buy fish & chips for two persons
Irish money came yesterday.

poet Allen Ginsberg gave me the army knife
in New York City 1988.
it stayed with me as a good friend like Allen.

agile and sharp as an old star
the fountain pen, my soul, wrote many poems.

boundless chain of life—
with the magnifying glass I inspected insect eggs,
flower seeds and the future of our galaxy.

the sunglasses were great for looking
into a rainbow, a sundog
& above the sundog . . . another rainbow.

Now the time is ripe.
I dedicate you all to Mt. Croagh Patrick.
you are gone . . . good luck!

# Go Walk Mathematics

Suppose you walk 3 kms a day for 40 years.
3 kms x 365 days = 1,095 kms.
Forget the 95 kms.
1,000 kms x 40 years = 40,000 kms
40,000 kms = the length of the terrestrial equator
Therefore
Walking 3 kms a day for 40 years
You complete your circuit of the earth.

Suppose you walk 30 kms a day for 36 years.
30 kms x 365 days = 10,950 kms
10,950 kms x 36 years = 394,200 kms
This figure goes beyond the average distance
Between the earth & the moon 384,400 kms.
Therefore
Walking 30 kms a day for 36 years
You reach the moon.

# Lovely Spring Dawn
*Dedicated to Sei Shonagon, a woman writer of Japan, 10th-11th century*


Lovely spring dawn—cherries in mid-bloom.
April 8th, a Friday, Buddha's birthday.

At Gojo bridge on Kamo River
in Kyoto landed a corps of 1200 angels;
uniforms of black, chainsaws for wings.

Their flag announces: "Congratulations upon
the 1200th anniversary of Kyoto City."

Radio reports:
*"At 11:59 last night 1200 Japanese cartoonists
disappeared. Tokyo Metropolitan Police
are investigating."*

*"Mannalargenna, representing the
Aboriginal Government of Australia,
has proclaimed the end of woodchip exports
to Japan forever."*

6am
"Black Angels! Black Angels!" shouts the crowd
at Gojo bridge. The angels disperse in three directions,
to Maruyama Park, Shimogamo Shrine, and
the Imperial Palace. In procession, a mob of spectators,
police squads and TV crews follow.

7am

With chainsaws revving, "Black Angels" arrive
and cut down trees all the forests are gone.
Riot Police are called to the scene as "Angels"
destroy the ancient groves. Though well-trained
to fight revolutionary students, they're no match
for heavenly invaders. Petrified with awe
they fall back in despair as onlookers roar
with laughter, and shake with fear.


8am

Equipped with machineguns, the Ground Self-
Defense Force comes to the rescue — unable to
shoot they are instantly dazzled by "Black Angels"
eyes, so shiny and dopey. So away soldiers run,
flinging weapons behind them.


9am

*"Schoolchildren, all ages, go home right away!!!"*
shouts the School Board Director on the city P.A.


10am

From Misawa Air Base in Aomori, fighters and bombers
roar over FOSSA MAGNA. The Mayor of Kyoto calls
the Prime Minister of Japan and asks him to stop the
planes, now approaching Lake Biwa in formation.
The Mayor says: *"Even the U.S. Air Force spared*
*Nara & Kyoto, and what about all our other*
*tourist attractions?"* The air-strike team
turns back, to the north.

11am
Beijing radio flash:
*"April 8th, 5am Japan time, Kyoto forests were*
*invaded by 1200 angels in uniform black, no*
*heavenly wings, but chainsaws attached.*
*Their size & shape, quite like Japanese;*
*no facial expressions, no hint of gender."*

Noon report:
Stock markets of Tokyo & Osaka closed.

1pm
Authorities close all financial institutions,
stationing armed guards at every one.

2pm
The Prime Minister of Japan addresses citizens
on TV, saying: *"Please trust me and my government!*
*We'll do everything we can to get rid of 'Black Angels'!*
*Don't worry about rice and toilet paper! Don't*
*listen to rumors or pay attention to scare-mongers!*
*I've already given the U.N. Security Council a call."*

3pm
In Washington DC. the U.S. President sacks
NASA's Director-in-Chief for negligently
not preventing the "Black Angels" invasion.

4pm
New York City:
*"A unanimous decision by U.N. Security Council*
*to help protect Japan from 'Black Angels'.*

*Bankers, scientists & strategists on a U.N. Special*
*Inquiry Commission Task Force leave for Japan.*
*A P.K.O. force against space invaders, now*
*undergoing training in the Sahara Desert,*
*will deploy to Japan within 48 hours".*

5pm
Tokyo Metropolitan Police Dept. dismisses the missing
cartoonists' case as *"one of God's pranks"*.

6pm
Kyoto: Three spaceships land on tree stumps at
the Park, Shrine and Imperial Palace. All "Black
Angels" enter the spacecraft. Riot Police and GSDF
keep their distance. Cloudless sky, brilliant evening glow.

6pm
Sayaka calls Kaya

*"Kaya, how's it going? Can you believe today?*
*'Black Angels', 'Black Angels', I can't take any more.*
*And nobody knows who they are. Are they scarecrows?*
*Or riot police? The Self-Defense Force?*
*Their eyes are like glass, like marble, they say.*
*How can I sleep while they cut down the forests?*
*Why don't we attack their spaceships tonight?*
*You're a strong wrestler, I know some karate . . .*
*We're twelve, that's old enough to do something.*
*We shouldn't be controlled & babied by society. What???*
*What's wrong with your mom? Her eyes rolled up*
*& she foamed at the mouth? Take care of her. Kaya!*
*I'll talk to you tomorrow."*

April 9th, Saturday, 10am
A message from Franz Kafka, Czech President:

*"The Czech people and I extend our deep sympathy*
*regarding the damage & suffering you are experiencing.*
*We expect these hardships to pass quickly of course,*
*Japanese people being both adaptable and courageous . . . "*

Noon Report:
Japan's Inquiry Commission discloses
the following findings about "Black Angels":

*1) They seem to have originated from the Great Galaxy*
   *of Andromeda, M31, and escaped our surveillance*
   *with a time-lag device.*
*2) They may look like Japanese, but truly they are not!*
*3) They exhibit no gender features, nor sexuality.*
*4) They show no stages of development; no signs of aging.*
*5) Though greenery is their energy source, their stomachs*
   *can't digest plant matter directly. Chemically decomposed*
   *toilet-paper is best, with an intellectual or artistic flavor.*
   *Therefore, their optimal diet is comic-book*
   *made of toilet paper.*
*6) The 1200 cartoonists disappeared from Tokyo to work*
   *at "Black Angels" factories in Kyoto.*
*7) "Black Angels" must have targeted Japan*
   *as the largest consumer of trees world-wide. Trees to*
   *woodchips to toilet paper to comic books. Comic books!*
   *—An industry with highest world-wide profits.*
*8) Whether or not to force the "Black Angels"*
   *to leave Japan has not yet been finally decided.*

1pm
The Finance Ministry announces:
*"April 11th Monday, from 9am, all financial institutions,
stock markets too, will be open for business as usual."*

2pm
The New York market lists the U.S. dollar at 360 yen.

3pm
The U.N. Special Inquiry Commission Task Force,
arriving at Narita, calls Japan *"defeatist'*
and warns against unilateral negotiation
with "Black Angels", saying *"this planet cannot
recognize sexless, ageless citizens".*

4pm
Too much excitement at a soccer game
injures 1200 fans at Shimizu City near Mt. Fuji.

6pm TV interview, from Kyoto's Tourist Information Center:
*"Yes, that's right. At first almost everyone was canceling,
but now we're flooded with reservations,
from within Japan and overseas. Seems angels
are of interest to everyone,"*
*"Skyscrapers, sight-rapers, more hotels!'*

9pm Sayaka phones Kaya:

*"Kaya, what's up? How's your mom? Just sleeping?
I walked all day. I saw everything. No trees
at parks, temples or schools. All trees cut down
to go to factories. Factories! I said spaceship factories!*

*Where trees turn to woodchips, to paper, and then*
*to toilet paper and comics, and more comics!*
*And then they eat them! That's dinner for celestial*
*people! Talk about metamorphosis!"*

Sayaka continues—

*"I went to Shijo-Kawaramachi in the afternoon.*
*It was full of young people, reading manga comics,*
*absent-minded, empty-headed, giggling and pointing*
*meaninglessly. I thought I must have been dreaming!"*

*"No, Kaya, wait, there's more. I came home*
*and found Grandpa all upset, stroking the tree-stumps*
*in our empty yard & moaning. Ok Kaya, I want to*
*see you, see all our friends. I want to get together*
*and hold hands."*

*Oh no! It's Grandpa, he's wet his pants.*
*Don't cry Grandpa, I'll help you. Kaya, bye!*

April 10th, Sunday; 7am
Kyoto Electric blames "Black Angels"
for frequent power blackouts during the night.

8am
Authorities monitor "Black Angels" movements
towards surrounding mountains—Hiei, Kurama,
and Atago.

Noon
Japan's Inquiry Commission discloses "Black Angels"
attack now spreading across the nation to:

1) Shiretoko Peninsula Reserve
2) Mt. Shirakami Beech Forest
3) West Kanto Mountain Zone (water source of Greater Tokyo)
4) Nagano Winter Olympic Site
5) Horyuji Temple
6) Himeji Castle
7) Yakushima Virgin Forest

7pm
Kyoto blacks out. Spaceships are self-powered.

At Sayaka's house, a small fire burns in the treeless
garden. Short-wave radio picks up a baseball game.
Darkness grows, stars shine above. Everyone is silent,
looking up and beyond, hearing radio noise,
listening to the fire. Jupiter to the east,
Orion over the western horizon. Big Dipper,
Arcturus and Spica make an arch overhead.

8pm
Japan's Prime Minister speaks:

*"This afternoon "Black Angels" were observed near*
*the following nuclear power stations. And later,*
*four spaceships floating above the plants:*

*1) Tomari, Hokkaido*
*2) Rokkasho, Aomori*
*3) Tokai, Ibaragi*
*4) Monju, Fukui*

*Therefore, all persons over 70 and under 10 years of age*
*living within a 50 km radius must evacuate now!*
*Please move to a 'Safe Zone'."*

9pm
Sayaka phones Kaya:

*"Hi Kaya, how are you? Your mum?*
*In our treeless garden we're watching the fire.*
*Such a gorgeous starry heaven above!*
*Do you know Jupiter? My dad taught it to me.*

*And I saw Io, too. Yes, one of the moons of*
*Jupiter. At first, we found it through binoculars,*
*then I could see it with my naked eyes!*
*Hey! This blackout's just great!*
*Kaya, try it yourself! A big star in the eastern*
*sky, golden yellow, not twinkling . . . Yes, that's it!*
*Next, find Io, a moon of Jupiter! You've got it!*
*Yaaay!!!"*

*"The bugs are chirping, bats are flying. But*
*how long can this last? Garden violets*
*now in full bloom won't last long without*
*shady trees. Where will bush warblers*
*sing* ho ho ke kyo? *Without trees, without*
*forests, there'll be no dragonflies, no beetles,*
*no frogs, no deer, no bear, and probably*
*no seasons! No, an earth without trees*
*we can't call home, only a world of concrete*
*junk, a ruin . . .*

Sayaka continues—

*"Sorry, I'm complaining, not listening to you!*
*I need to see your face & all our school friends.*

*We've got to do something. Can we meet*
*somewhere tomorrow, have you any ideas?*
*Let's climb Mt. Hiei and confront "Black*
*Angels" there! Get everyone we know!*
*Wear bright colors, not uniforms, please!*
*We'll start at dawn! Get some sleep!*

> *Blue Sky Doll!*
>> *Blue Sky Doll!*
>>> *Bring Blue Sky Tomorrow!"*

# Venerate Three Treasures

"BUDDHAM SARANAM GACCHAMI
DHAMMAM SARANAM GACCHAMI
SANGHAM SARANAM GACCHAMI"
       "WE VENERATE BUDDHA
       WE VENERATE DHARMA
       WE VENERATE SANGHA"

This year, this autumn
To save all sentient beings
Buddha Shakyamuni sends Boddhisattva Manjusri
To Prince Shotoku's country Japan
To Wakasa Bay, north of Kyoto.

"WHO ARE YOU?"
WHERE HAVE YOU COME FROM?"

| | |
|---|---|
| 15 billion years ago | Big Bang |
| 4.5 billion years ago | Creation of the Earth |
| 3 billion years ago | Life begins |
| 0.5 million years ago | Peking man |
| 2557 years ago | Buddha Shakyamuni |
| 1994 years ago | Jesus Christ |
| 1442 years ago | Prince Shotoku |
| 49 years ago | Hiroshima bombing |
| 7 years ago | Chernobyl disaster |

HOPELESSLY SQUATTING,
YOU, BIRD-MAN IN THE CAGE.
WHEN COULD YOU BE LIBERATED?"

This year, this autumn
To save all sentient beings
Boddhisattva Manjusri
Comes to Japan, comes to Wakasa Bay.

Now standing on the beach of Wakasa Bay
Boddhisattva Manjusri
Takes the place of a fast breeder reactor
Extinguishes the hell's flame of Plutonium
With his own blood & tears,
And illuminates the gloomy world
With his boundless compassion.

Therefore Boddhisattva Manjusri's fast breeder reactor
Produces no radioactive contamination
Produces no nuclear explosion
Produces no atomic bomb.

Illuminated by Boddhisattva Manjusri's compassion
Human beings together with all sentient beings
Repeat their birth & death
& keep their lives happy & in peace
In the coming century & beyond it
Until planet Earth's last day.

Though . . . red blood & black tears
Trickling from the ringed skulls of
Hiroshima, Nagasaki & Chernobyl
Will tint the horizon
Until planet Earth's last day.
This year, this autumn

To save all sentient beings
Boddhisattva Manjusri
Comes to Japan, comes to Wakasa Bay.

"WE VENERATE BUDDHA
WE VENERATE DHARMA
WE VENERATE SANGHA"
    "BUDDHAM SARANAM GACCHAMI
    DHAMMAM SARANAM GACCHAMI
    SANGHAM SARANAM GACCHAMI"

*1. Prince Shotoku (572-621 AD) introduced Buddhism into Japan.*

*2. The title of the poem comes/rom the first constitution of Japan which was proclaimed by Prince Shotoku.*

*3. "WHO ARE . . . & "HOPELESSLY . . ." are age-old children songs of Japan.*

*4. Who knows why the fast breeder reactor was named after Boddhisattva Manjusri?*

# Anyday

As the sun set on a mid-winter day
Along the Japan sea coast
I visited Mihama nuclear plants
& the fast breeder reactor "Mohju"
In Wakasa Bay, north of Kyoto,
Where nuclear plants are congregated.

The next morning I was standing
On a platform of Tsuruga railway station.
Dark clouds tumbling, snow drifting
Birds fluttering in the chilly gusts of wind.

Next moment—
        GWOOON    BALI    BALI!
        A GREAT EXPLOSION!

        A blinding FLASH and a deafening n o i s e.

Oh, my Buddha!

I found myself trembling in a cold sweat
                        with a painful shock.

Thank goodness!
The explosion was but a thunderclap
Not of a bursting atomic energy plant
YET.

Four days later
A big earthquake struck Kobe
Killing more than six thousand
people.

# Star Bikki

A myth—a new star is born!
There are teeny, tiny six thousand stars
In the solar system, the Minor planets or Asteroids
Which turn around the sun, day & night.

Somebody discovered a new one
& named it Bikki after my friend's name.

Bikki Sunazawa—
Born in Hokkaido as Ainu
All his life he was carving
Something in the empty sky with his chisel
Something in wood with his soul
Like his grandfathers.

Oct 1988, his health was not good—
On one beautiful afternoon
I took my canoe & visited his studio.

Looking into my eyes, he asked
"Nanao, is the twenty-first century really coming?"

Tired out. Jan 1989, he said
"Bye bye" to this world.

And one day he metamorphosed into a tree,
His favorite one, an Ezo spruce in his garden.

The tree grows higher & higher above the clouds.
Today you find him in the solar system
As one of the Minor planets.

Hi Star Bikki Congratulations!

Do you know about your new identity card?

| | |
|---|---|
| 1. Registered number: | 5372. |
| 2. Star Name: | Bikki |
| 3. Temporary number: | 1987 WS. |
| 4. Discoverer: | Kin Marudate |
| | Kazuo Watanabe. |
| 5. Discovery spot: | Kitami |
| | Hokkaido, Japan. |

Hi Star Bikki! Nowadays
What are you carving?
\What songs are you singing?
What kind of Sake are you drinking?

Hi star Bikki! Sometime
Send me a postcard
Decorated full of stars!

# With Left Hand

With left hand,
I try to write.

A. B. C. D. E. F. G . . .
Wow, I made it!

1. 2. 3. 4. 5. 6. 7 . . .
Wow, I made it!

A summer evening
I met the child

We jump, fly, dance
On the rocks in a calm cove.

We never ask
Who are you
Where are you from.

Jump, fly, dance
Jump, fly, dance.

As the sun set
We said bye, bye.

With left hand
I can write.

Now let's start
With right hand!

JULY 7, 1995 *Denman Island Pacific Northwest.*

# Perennial Treasures

October morning sky, cirrus floating on.
In my friend's narrow garden
At the outskirts of Nagoya City, Japan
I found a loofah hanging on the vine, 40 cm long
& a small rice paddy, cement-walled, perfectly ripened.
Today we'll begin with
  harvesting rice crop
  harvesting happiness.

Tomorrow I'll start walking with my friends
Along Nagara River: a two week trip, about 225 km.

Far, far south of this city
Somewhere in a peaceful village
An 89 year-old woman is living by herself.
She toddles about her kitchen and grumbles:
  "Before going far away
  I want to clean up my home & garden."

1914 outburst of nearby volcano, Sakura-jima.
1945 air raid by American Air Force.
Living almost one century
Her niche becomes a junkyard
  —books, clothes, so many kinds of utensils.
In her garden, plenty of plants
  —camellia, azalea, camphor tree
pampas grass, fern & moss,

And nests of snakes, spiders, earthworms
& mushrooms

Fine visitors from Siberia last winter
          —Bohemian waxwings.
I fancy that the richness of her garden
Equals that of the Royal Botanical Garden in London
And me also
Keeping my stuff in so many niches;
          —Asia, N. America, Oceania . . .
          —Books, music tapes, clothes, ice-axe . . .
Someday, empty handed
I wish to leave this world behind.

Wait a moment!

By the beginning of the 21st century
Japan, my mother land will be
The number one junkyard on planet Earth
          —Tokyo tower, Nagara River dam,
          Fast breeder reactor Monju
          & Nagano Winter Olympics.
Leaving such a mess behind
Who can die in peace?

Far, far east of this city
From the Sierra Nevada, N. America
Poet Gary Snyder sends me a letter:
          "I'm leaving for the Himalayas tomorrow morning.
          I'll say hello to Chomolungma for you!"

With the Indian landmass moving northward slowly but steadily
Chomolungma must stand on tiptoe these days.
And me also—straightening my backbone
Against the northerly wind
I start walking along the Nagara River tomorrow.

# Good Night Copernicus

Good morning!
Incredible deep blue sky over snow mountains!
Hang your bedding and washing in the sun!

Winter solstice . . . New Year's Day
And tomorrow . . . January 3rd . . .
The planet Mercury reaches its greatest elongation eastward
About 20° east of the sun . . . astronomers announce.
These days I stay with my friends in Noto Peninsula
Along the Sea of Japan.
Almost every day and night here come snowstorms
Because cold Siberian air merges with warm water of Black Current.
Therefore no-one trusts tomorrow; but today is blue sky.

With five binoculars, with four men and a dog
I climb to western hilltop at evening.
Snow deep and hard.  Sky all clear.
Sun leaves its halo on the horizon.
A golden oval disk hangs at the center of heaven.

Polished with graceful purple dark
And brightening moon's flame
The pure snow shames even diamonds.

| 15:20pm | Venus |
| 5:40pm | Mercury |
| 6:00pm | Saturn, Pleiades, Orion, Cygnus, Lyra |
| | and two artificial satellites. |

Incredible but true . . .
Copernicus in his lifetime
Never saw Mercury.

Around midnight
I get into my sundried pajamas
And creep into my sundried bedding.

Yes, the heliocentric system is perfect . . .
Now I jump on the zodiac light as my broom
And dream back to the sun's corona.

Goodnight Copernicus, have a good sleep!

# Me, a Smuggler

1)  A February morning. Taipei Airport, Formosa
    A bush warbler calling me.
    I crawled into a nearby wood to see the warbler up close.
    On the aircraft, approaching Osaka, Japan
    I felt somebody crawling on my chest
    Instantaneously my fingertips caught a tick.
    With a magnifying glass I was glad to see
    A new comrade—the tick on my palm.
    Seeing the tick, an old lady next to me
    Screamed wildly.
    Soon after we landed, I released my tiny friend
    In the wood outside the airport,
    Saying "Come back sometime"

2)  One autumn evening
    From a mountain village of Japan
    I arrived at my friend's apartment
    In Manhattan, New York City.
    When I opened my backpack to pick up a souvenir
    Here, strange hitchhikers crawling out
    —one, two, three, four, five, six, seven—
    Shiny green skunk-bugs
    One by one, heading for outer space
    They flew out of window.

3)  Shrikes keep their left-overs
    —butterfly, grasshopper, spider—

On sharp twigs as preserves.
One Autumn day in the hills outside Tokyo
I gathered these well-dried preserves
And carried them to San Francisco
As the best souvenirs I could imagine.


4) Twinkle, twinkle—to whom do all stars twinkle?
One summer night I offered the Southern Crown
To a graceful lady named Sally
Somewhere in the Southern Rockies.
Another summer night I presented the same constellation
To a bright-eyed woman named Kaya in Okinawa
Ten or twenty summers later
I visited two ladies living in California
Sally, blessed with many friends
Kaya, blessed with five children.
They are each constructing their own constellations.


5) Me, a smuggler!
Carrying an enormous backpack on my shoulders
Together with Prince Okuni of Japan
And Kokopelli of North America
Someday I will smuggle

| | |
|---|---|
| Coyote | from the Rocky Mountains |
| Glacier | from Alaska |
| Desert | from Sahara |
| Virgin Forest | from Tasmania |
| Blue coral | from Ishigaki, Okinawa |
| Fresh green leaves | from Japanese forest |

To a newborn constellation.

6) As lightly as the wind
   As energetically as the sun
   I smuggle my merchandise
   Beyond all boundaries
   Beyond the void.

   Don't call my trade-mark, "Poetry"!

1. *Bush warbler: Cetfia diphone*

2. *Shrikes: Family Laniidae*

3. *Prince Okunv.Also known as Doctor Big Black, medicineman of ancient Japanese mythology.*

4. *Kokopelli: Seed offering spirit of Hopi.*

# Doctor Big Black Coming

In the olden days
A barefoot, grass root doctor
Big Black was roaming in Japan.
Carrying on his shoulders a big sack
Full of medicinal herbs and wisdom.
One day he found a white rabbit
Suffering much with skin bitten off
By a demon's teeth.
The good doctor immediately rescued the rabbit.

Today, to rescue an endangered endemic species
Amami Black rabbit
Threatened by the construction of a golf course.
He comes back to Japan
Accompanied by the eternal Miss Universe
Princess Kaguya.

One day, October 1995
A bamboo raft was floating
At Nagara River Dam site.
On the raft—

> Doctor Big Black, Princess Kaguya,
> Pluto, Master mason Three Five Jack,
> Kokopelli, Boddhisattva Manjusri,
> and Nanao Sakaki.

These seven wise people came
To an agreement that

Nagara River Dam should be preserved forever
As a memorial to the monumental silliness
Of Japanese in the twentieth century.

Pluto the King of Hades who was so much
Impressed by the unhealthiness of recent dead,
Started for the above world
To consult with Doctor Big Black.
He was accompanied by
The Master mason. Three Five Jack.
In Kagoshima City
They arrived at Nishida stone bridge,
A masterpiece built by Three Five Jack
One hundred fifty years ago.
Finding out that for more traffic capacity
The old stone bridge will be demolished shortly,
Pluto turned back to Hades
Never looking behind.

As a volunteer with Doctor Big Black,
The humpbacked flute player,
A spirit of North America, Kokopelli,
Who gives away cereals and songs
Will visit Japan soon
To cheer up Japanese who are suffering much
with Kobe earthquake,
Sarin attack in Tokyo subway,
A serious accident at fast breeder reactor Monju
and Nagano Winter Olympics
Kokopelli carries on his shoulders
A huge sack of flower seeds
Which will bloom tomorrow as fairy tales.

# Crystal Clock

"Good morning, Ho, Hoke, Kyo!
With a familiar song a bush warbler wakes me up.

"Have a good journey, Ho, Hoke, Kyo!"
The same warbler sends me off.

A mountain I walk in
With two friends
Looks so charming today.

Dianthus, tiger lily, the rose of Sharon and Canna.
We follow a flowery trail.
Higher & higher . . .

By wayside in fog, white lily flowers line up.
The canyon is covered with silk trees in full bloom.
Thundering over the mountain
A winter wren sings.

After crawling through bushes & crossing rivulets
We reach an abandoned copper mine.

"Eureka!"
Under a rocky ledge
There . . . tiny, shiny crystals peer out.

Born at unknown depth
Between light & darkness of Mother Earth
Crystals wait voiceless.

From the Planet Earth, one day,
This star-dust must fall down to the Milky Way.
With wide-open eyes & empty minds
We pick up transparent star-dust
One, two, three . . .

Angelic play over,
We relax in the ancient oak forest.

"Eureka!"
From the canopy of tree tops
Down to the underbrush
Sharp crystal sun-beams
Peer down
One, two, three.

This is a crystal palace.
On the facade of the palace
Hangs a crystal clock.

Listen to ticking of the clock!

For bird: bug, song & wing
For animal & man: a scented breeze
For tree & grass: flower & fruit
For crystal: a solar spectrum
Living with stars
Here & now.

Listen to ticking of the clock!

JULY 1996 *Mt. Sobo, Japan*

# In the Twenty-First Century

1) In the twenty-first century
   We're going to have   no principles alone
                          no practices alone
                          no backroom negotiations
                          no deceptions
                          no bullies
                          no conspiracies
                          no fixed matches
                          no halo effects
                          no favored employment
                          no medals

2) In the twenty-first century
   We're going to have   no homeless
                          no gangsters
                          no personalities
                          no big names
                          no living national treasure
                          no Nobel Prize
                          no World Cultural Heritage
                          no mental hospitals
                          no prisons
                          no death penalties

3) In the twenty-first century
   We're going to have   no paper diapers
                          no toilet paper
                          no newspaper inserts
                          no direct mail

no weekly magazines
no comic books
no wood chips
no imported wood
no refugee camps
no P(eace) K(eeping) O(peration)

4)   In the twenty-first century
    We're going to have   no atopic dermatitis
                         no chemical seasonings
                         no lung cancer
                         no smoking
                         no alcoholism
                         no diabetes
                         no gourmets
                         no diets
                         no starvation
                         no paradise

5)   In the twenty-first century
    We're going to have   no computer games
                         no vending machines
                         no health drinks
                         no AIDS
                         no pinball games
                         no Karaoke
                         no cell phone
                         no designer brands
                         no G 7 summits
                         no guided missiles

6)   In the twenty-first century
    We're going to have   no microwave oven
                         no air-conditioning

no TV shows
no marine shows
no jingles
no baseball fever
no Olympics
no internet
no space stations
no tetrapods

7) In the twenty-first century
We're going to have   no mineral water
no chlorinated tap water
no exhaust fumes
no dump trucks
no agricultural chemicals
no abandoned farming villages
no homes for the aged
no Santa Claus
no inheritance
no pet graveyards

8) In the twenty-first century
We're going to have   no big construction companies
no corruption
no estuary dams
no bullet trains
no super highways
no pH-neutral detergent
no bright city lights
no industrial waste disposal sites
no river sludge
no acid rain.

9) In the twenty-first century
   We're going to have   no sales tax
                               no golf courses
                               no National Foundation Day
                               no Valentine's Day
                               no cram schools
                               no dropouts
                               no elite
                               no eternal progress of science
                               no Chernobyl
                               no Hiroshima & Nagasaki

10) In the twenty-first century
   We're going to have   no smile on children's faces
                               no bird songs
                               no earthworms in the fields
                               no dragonfly nymphs in the river
                               no mushrooms in the forests
                               no fish in the coral reefs
                               no sun in the deserts
                               no cloud shadows on the ground
                               no color in the rainbows
                               no stars in the Milky Way

11) In the twenty-first century
                               Everything will disappear
                               From the planet Earth
                               But somewhere—
                               Wind speaks—
                               Somewhere in the twenty-first century
                               Romeo and Juliet are alive.
                               Romeo and Juliet are alive.

OCTOBER 1996 *At the Cemetery of*
*The United Nations' Army 1950-1953 Pusan, Korea*

# Don't Cry Yoshino River

Somewhere on the Water Planet
Somewhere in Yaponesia
Somewhere in a rice-rich country
Along the Median Tectonic Line

> There is holy water.
> People call it a river:
> People call it Yoshino River.

Earth's muscle—the mountains high.
Earth's bloodlines—the gorges deep.

The Yoshino River
Gathers snow, rain and beech tree sap,
Cascades numberless falls, and
For a short while
Hanging in the terracing rice paddies
Reflects beautifully thousands of moons
Through late spring nights.

In the olden days
When the Yoshino River was dreaming
The twenty-first century
A golden wooden-horse was crossing
In a desert of concrete blocks and plastic trees.

A mysterious figure,
With an attache case and a portable phone,
Was sitting uprightly on that golden saddle.

Today, the Yoshino River
Is a flow of spirits
Offering generously
Its beauty, its strength and its richness
To all beings.

At the end of an epic journey
The water is returning
To the Mother Ocean
Now and always.

Look there!
At the estuary
A golden monolithic dam
Rises up!

Under the foot of the magic dam
All disappears . . .
From the tidal flat        the fiddler crab
From the beach           the whimbrel
From the binoculars       the osprey
From the future          the birdwatcher.

Living in his concrete cave
Third Stone Age man,
Just like a fiddler crab,
Brandishes triumphantly
His one-sided tremendous claw.
What destiny awaits him tomorrow?

Don't cry Yoshino River!
    You are holy water!
    People call you a river!
    People call you Yoshino River!

Don't cry Yoshino River!

# How to Live on the Planet Earth

Dwell in the neighborhood
Of stars & rainbows.

With donkey's ears
Listen to the wind whispering.

With monkey's limbs
Hang around mountains & rivers.

Be rich in the wild life.
Waste not, want not in human life.

Don't work without hearty sweat.

From afar
Ah, one of my dear friends arrives.
Let's have a daikon dish,
Home-made Sake & songs.

Shadow's shadows—
Supermarket, hospital & bank—
What a perfect sight.

Under the horizon of the void
The authorities set.

The Sun & the moon
To look up forever.

# A Sweet Comet

1.)    An unexpected comet!
In the morning
To my humble retreat in a snow mountain
Arrived a package from a friend of south Japan
Contents—brown sugar, ginger
& purplish sweet potatoes.

2.)    On these days in the village where I stay
Trees shed their leaves already.
Bears hide in their caves.
Monkeys move away to the warmer zone.
Villagers stay inside houses with TV program.
Me, only love to ramble in wintry air,
Turquoise blue sky on my head
A little snow under my boot.

3.)    As the lunch for an ever hungry ghost
I try quite enterprising meal.
Boil millet first.
Add grated sweet potatoes & gingers.
At the end, put more than enough brown sugar into the pot.

4.)    I taste a spoonful of the soup—
Another unexpected comet!
Instantaneously a pleasant surprise runs through
My whole body from top to toe.
Sweet, clean, sharp, in all exquisite!
Too good to swallow in one breath!

5.) From the depth of my spirit
    A strange commotion stirs up my blood & veins.
    Now the sweet comet carries me far away.
    I realize my body is floating in the air,
    Looking down the mountain range & villages,
    Covering one thousand miles over the lands & the oceans.
    I'm now the sweet comet itself
    Tailing a long shiny broom behind.

6.) Sure, you are!
    But it is too delicious to be eaten by one man.
    Why don't you share it around the world?
    Back to the ground again
    I carry the pot in my hands,
    Step on the icy trail
    To my neighborhood
    Shouting "Taste the sweet comet!"
    "Taste the flying sweet comet please!"

7.) Next morning
    I look at Comet Hale-Bopp in the twilight.

# April First 1997

1.) The Environmental Agency of Tokyo government
    disclosed the worst one hundred tap-waters of Japan.

2.) The Defense Agency will replace the soldiers of
    the Self Defense Forces of Japan with foreign legions.

3.) To evade the financial catastrophe,
    for all money business offices
    the Ministry of Finance ordered
    the use of Fox's flower money of cherry tree
    as the currency.

4.) A Copernican revolution!
    The Ministry of International Trade & Industry
    decided to move the general policy
    from the extravagant, ever-growing economy
    to the stable growth with exchange & barter.

5.) Before the year 2997
    the Ministry of Agriculture & Fishery
    will bring back the whole afforestation
    of Sugi, Japanese cedar into the perfect
    natural forests, & the revitalized woods
    will be the eternal sanctuary for the wild beings.

6.) For the terracing rice paddy farmers
    the Cultural Agency will offer
    the title of National Human Treasure
    & enough money to live on for their elegant lives.

7. )  The Ministry of Construction who
       already filled up Tokyo Bay
       with earth & rocks of Mt. Fuji
       will build up another Mt. Fuji
       with ferro concrete for a tourism complex.

8.)   To make schooling more efficient
       the Ministry of Education wants
       that all grammar schools & junior high schools
       should be reorganized into three categories
       A, Elite course. B, Robot course. C. Dropout course.

9.)   So many times Pluto, the king of Hades asked
       the Ministry of Public Welfare
       to save miserable dead in Hades
       who are suffering with Japan-oriented mental disease.
       Today, the Ministry starts selecting
       ten elite government officials
       to send to the king Pluto.

10.)  For Japanese politicians who are
       the most reliable & cleanest politicians in the world,
       the Ministry of Justice granted that
       as an exception
       they can get bribes on April 1st.

11.)  The U.N. Security Council is inclined to believe
       that April Fools should be prohibited
       lest the Global Guerrillas take it as their tactics.

# Bye-Bye Allen Ginsberg

For a start, try what you can make it!
Don't try what you can't!

> On the golden eagle mountain trail
> There hang bell-shaped purple flowers
> Of deadly nightshade, a hallucinogenic.

"Me, a pale green gourd man.
How can I survive?"

"Sit in the outside of your meditation!
Take off, leaving your brain behind!
The world is just a dream, be crazy!"

> Who ate up the sprout
> Of sorrel, my favorite vegetable,
> —monkey, deer, wild boar or bear?

"When you are thirsty for love,
Cry in the arch of your foot!
On a big day—
Laugh at the bottom of your navel!"

> There, the silence thunders in heaven.
> Here, titmice flush in wood.

> It is five minutes to eternity.
> Hi, spring wind
> When will you return?

1997

# Life Goes On & On

On a chestnut tree
Chestnut flowers bloom.

On a chestnut tree
The sun hangs down.

On a chestnut tree
Chestnut fruits ripen.

On a chestnut tree
Cold showers drizzle.

On a chestnut tree
Chestnut fruits fall.

On a chestnut tree
Snowflakes linger.

On a chestnut tree
The spring wind returns.

On a chestnut tree
Chestnut flowers bloom.

On a chestnut tree
Life goes on & on.

June 1997 *Kanto Basin, Japan*

# A Prayer

As a species
Homo sapiens is overbearing one.

As a nation
Japan is haughty one.

As a human being
I'm not unassuming.

Let's walk back to our dumping ground.

# Crane Dance

*(musicians, chorus on stage; crane, hunter behind curtain)*
*(conchhorn, music starts)*

Chorus:    By whom turns our galaxy?
                To whom turns our solar system?
                For whom turns four seasons?
                It is vernal equinox today;
                Sun rises due East.
                Sun sets due West.
                Day and night are equal.

Hunter:    (comes out, looks around) Good morning.
                How wonderful—spring! I am a hunter,
                an honorable bowman of the Anasazi,
                an ancient people. I love this land,
                full of cosmic space, vast and profound.
                This is an excellent place to be born,
                to live and to die. *(he looks upward)*
                Oh, high in the sky I hear loud trumpets,
                resonant, a blaring call. Yes, here comes
                a flock of cranes flying northward. These
                sandhill cranes are of ancient and noble
                lineage like us.

*(a crane appears, dancing)*

Chorus:    Look, their elegant and fervent flight.
                Necks straight out in front,

Feet trailing behind tailing,
Wingbeat regular and steady,
Slow downstroke, rapid upstroke alternately.

*(the crane leaves)*

Hunter:    So, we Anasazi admire you very much and never
           hurt you. Now I wish to celebrate your voyage
           with my arrow, *(he shoots without aiming)*

Chorus:    What cursed arrow you loose!
           Look, one of the cranes deadly wounded,
           Falling and falling to the ground.
           In spite of your good heart,
           You commit a great sin against your people.
           As an outcast you must wander forever!

Hunter:    *(showing agony)* Sweet and rich, oh Mother Earth!
           Why do you desert me in such a a cruel way?
           *(suddenly he becomes calm)* A voice! Listen my
           heart! Alive! I must rescue the crane first,
           however horrible my fate would be.

Chorus:    Searching for the pitiable crane,
           He walks and walks day and night,
           On mesa of morning glow crimson,
           Up ridge in evening blizzard,
           With coyote of moonlit canyon.

Hunter:    At last I come to the Rio Grande! This sacred
           river, this great Rio, cutting south through
           lava mesa. This gorge, this chasm seems a
           trail well-trodden by cranes.

Chorus:    The sun is already up.
           But down in the gorge, within the abyss,
           Night, fog, dream still lingering.
           Deep enough for your sin!
           Long enough for your sorrow.

Hunter:    Near the bottom, why there is something
           steaming, upright streaming!

Chorus:    Yes, something hidden,
           Go and find it.
           Walk down the gorge.
           Something within the abyss
           Waits for you in hiding. Go!

Chorus:    Here is a hot spring,
           Hidden behind large rocks.
           A Gift of the Mother Earth Miraculous.
           Gaze through the mist
           From the spring rising, stand by!

Crane:     *(appears)* I am the crane you are seeking.

Hunter:    What amazing beauty nature offers!
           Then you are spirit of crane?

Crane:     Yes, and No. In truth I am pure spirit;
           deathless, untouchable, flowing as an unbroken
           river of love. Therefore, I can be a peaceful
           crane, a fair lady . . .

Chorus:    You lovely, brave hunter of truth!
              What destiny brought you down here?
              The crane, the lady, the spirit
              All in All.
              Now she starts dancing.
              Her love pure and holy.
              Who can resist her invitation?

Crane:      *(after long ecstatic dancing)* By our dancing,
              by this celestial ceremony, I have conceived
              a new life: am Pregnant. But now I must
              catch up with my folk, the Sandhill Crane.
              In the autumn, when day and night are once
              more equal, I will return with our child.

Chorus:    Before long, he shall be a great leader of people.
              In the age to come, there shall be
              Drought, famine, epidemic, war—
              Endless, endless suffering.
              Everybody starving for love!
              Everybody thirsting for faith!
              But he, your son, will lead people
              Into the world of Spirit,
              Into the eternal dancing of Love.

              Look! She rises to leave!
              Now riding the southerly breeze she flies upriver!
              Fare thee well!
              The hunter stands on the edge,
              Sending her off without a word,
              Crystal dew whining in his eyes,
              Fare thee well.

# Snow Woman

STAGE SETTING:  A chair, upstage center.

CHARACTERS:     *Mac*—Middle-aged man in overalls.

                      *Snow Woman*—With a white mask and a white robe

                      *The Cleaner*—Middle-aged woman with an apron.

LIGHTING:       Daytime, evening, morning.

MUSIC:          Preferably Japanese Noh theater music will be played. Conch horn, bell, flutes/percussion.

Time:           Ideally 30 min.

*(Musicians sit upsstage right. Opening music—2 min.)*

Mac:    *(shaking snow from his head and his shoulders)*
For three days snowing! For three days constipation!
Going to the outhouse I must wade through three feet
of snow each time.
*(He sits on the chair, biting his thumb)*

And—so much bad luck these days. My wife deserted me
a month ago. The electricity stopped a week ago; so no TV,
no radio. The telephone doesn't work. My firewood almost
gone. My provisions scanty too. No more coffee.
This is the last whiskey.
*(He stands up and throws empty bottle out the window)*

And—the worst—my truck completely broke down
yesterday. How can I survive this severe winter?
Should I hibernate like bears?
*(He goes back to the chair)*

And—the whole world seems constipated too.
No solution for air pollution, for the energy shortage and
for nuclear war. No way to escape at all.
(*He goes to the window*)

And—here three feet of snow. I hate snow, that horrible,
terrible, merciless stuff, covering everything with ghostly
white color, and confining me in such a miserable mountain
cabin. What a nightmare!
(*He sits on the chair*)

It's getting dark. A coyote? Looking for my female dog?
I'm sorry. She is gone with my wife.

Voice:   Good evening!
         (*Mac jumps up from the chair*)

Voice:   Good evening!

Mac;     Who are you?

Voice:   Snow Woman.

Mac:     No thank you, Snow—. Are you Snow Woman?

SW:      As you see—
         (*She enters the stage*)

Mac:     No kidding! Who are you? Why are you here?
         Where do you come from? My name is Mac.
         Tell me your name—please!

SW:      I am Snow Woman.

Mac:    O.K.! But I have no food or bed for you.

SW:     Don't waste time on trifles. I have something for you.
        Are you ready?

Mac:    Ready for what? Why? For what reason?

SW:     No reason is the best reason. I have come to teach you
        snow dancing.

Mac:    No thank you! Spare me—please! I'm utterly tired of snow.
        Enough snow, too much snow already.
        *(He goes to the chair)*

SW:     Don't complain! I wonder—are you master of your life
        or not?

Mac:    No, —I'm a fool.

SW:     You are not a fool if you realize you are a fool.
        *(Mac jumps up from the chair and goes behind it)*

        Now listen to my truth. I am Life-giving Spirit. Snow is
        one of my myriad shapes. Blizzard, avalanches, rainbow,
        thunderbolt, hurricane, earthquake, volcano, sea current—
        all my manifestations.

        And, to be initiated into my dancing, you must be utterly
        purified first. Therefore, I had many miseries arranged
        for you this winter.

Mac:    Thank you so much. But I'm not a pious man.
        Why did you pick me out?

SW: NO-HUMAN-BEING-CAN-TOUCH-
THIS-INVIOLABLE-PLOT.
You are destined for the honorable distinction.

Mac: —Then what do you want?

SW: Watch the snow falling, and listen to my song!
*(Mac goes to the window)*

White-robed ptarmigan
Flies over winter glacier.
River otter slides down
Spring river bank.
Blue columbine blooms
In summer ravine.
Golden aspen glows
In autumn meadow.

Mountains, deserts, oceans—
The earth and Great Universe
All made of Spirit.
The Spirit gives color and sound
To every being.
As a being universal and individual
A person equals a snowflake.
Lovely snow!
Flake after flake
In the right place.

*(With Snow Woman's song, music gradually rises. Mac moves
his body, first awkwardly, then with flowing movement as
Snow Woman does. They dance together—3 min. Mac moves to
the chair and falls asleep. Snow Woman stands still.
"Lullaby music"—2 min.)*

Mac:    (*Mac wakes up*)
        Sun is rising, moon setting! At last no
        more snow! What a nightmare I had last night!
        Wasn't I crazy? Dancing with that strange woman!
        Was she a real being or my fantasy?—
        Where is she now?—There!
        (*He goes to her anxiously*)

        What? She is frozen, all ice!
        Even her fingers are icicles.
        (*She grabs his hand. Trembling and shivering he cries*)

        No! Ah, no! Help me! Spare me—please!
        (*He also becomes a frozen statue, first with agonized
        then ecstatic expression*)

The Cleaner:
        (*Humming "Mac the Knife", carrying her broom she enters the stage*)
        A rosy dawn. Two ravens circle high-with morning breeze.
        Three old cottonwoods stand still. Good start for the day.
        (*She sits in the chair*)

        At sunrise I clean the plaza for the neighborhood and for
        the tourists. I love my job, I'm proud of my broom.
        Yesterday's newspapers, leftover food, cigarette butts,
        whiskey bottles, scraps of dreams—all scattered here and
        there waiting for my broom.
        (*She starts sweeping*)

        The worst—look at those frozen statues! Many winter
        mornings I must clean up these strange dreamers.
        (*She goes to them*)

This is not paradise or El Dorado, but the plaza.
No leftover nightmare here. Wake up!

*(With her broom the cleaner tries to sweep them up, but she can't make it. She watches her broom then lets it fall down to the ground. Sitting on the chair, in a thoughtful pose, slowly the cleaner touches her cheek with her right forefinger—in the Kwan-yin posture of compassionate wisdom.)*

*(Smiling, she goes to the frozen dreamers again and hugs them tenderly. Mac starts moving, then Snow Woman becomes alive too. Dancing again with music—2 min.)*

*(The cleaner, with her broom, gradually chases them off. At the edge of the stage, music and actions stop suddenly. The cleaner and Mac stare at each other briefly. Music and actions resume.)*

The Cleaner:

Getting cloudy again. More snow coming, I'm sure.

*(Humming "Mac the Knife", carrying her broom, she walks offstage. Ending music, 1 min.)*

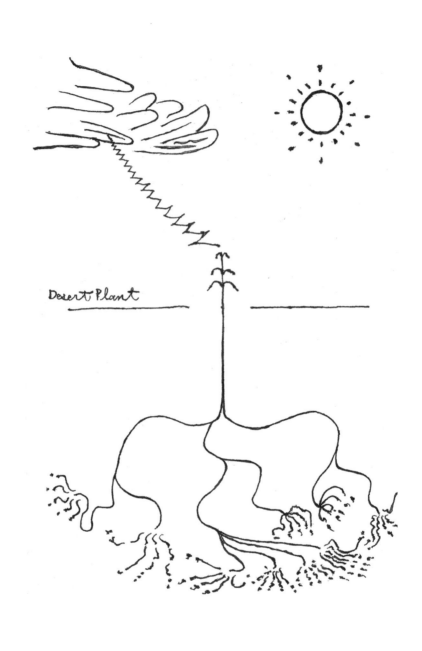

Desert Plant

# LATER POEMS

# A Dance of Coral

Me, coral —a miracle.
Born in warm ocean, grow and become a bone.
The bone changes into a stone,
       an island, a dream then the sun.
The sun transforms into wind, Buddha then God.
God metamorphoses into sea-weeds.
Sea-weeds raise a tiny blue planet, the earth.
The earth now brings up life on it.
At the end of journey the earth goes back to coral.

East China Sea.
Windy spring night.
Low clouds, high waves.
Me, coral—a miracle.
Extending my heart filled tentacles
I dance an eternal love.

Wind and waves
Standing on the thousand miles of Chinese coral wall
I dance an eternal love
In the name of an unknown being.

Here, life's spiral spinning
Where the earth and the world meet
Where a girl's smile melts down a hard rock
Where a boy's teardrops shine over the Indigo-Blue-Ocean.

Day by day rising tide and falling tide.
Offshore there runs an ocean river from the tropics.

The moon and stars circulating—every-night.
In a labyrinth of coral reef,
Human history circulating.
In a gorge of menses
Milky Way circulating.

Tears and smile. Me, coral—a miracle.
Digesting all circulating and flowing worlds I change them into
stone, into flowery silence.
—Every being could dance together—
        I sing a song without voice.

MARCH 1989 *Shiraho, Okinawa*

# Hula-Hoop

Under evening glow
I play hula-hoop with children
Turning our hips, bellybuttons & eyeballs.
Hi Hula-Hoop!

The garden turns, the sky turns
& the world turns.
Hi Hula-Hoop!

Turn, turn the planet earth
Until you fall down on the ground.
Hi Hula-Hoop!

From the top of an electric pole
Suddenly a voice drops, dry & cool,
"Kappon Kappon"!
Is that a mountain witch or a crow?

Behind western hill
A flaming disk jumps down with a "Bang!"
Is that a U.F.O. or the sun?

In twilight
Upon the southern sky wall
A golden heart climbs up & up.
Is that a dragon or the planet Jupiter?

At midnight blue dark
The hula-hoop lies on the ground,
Pleiades & Orion are up high. Now where is
Our star of the twenty-first century?

SEPTEMBER 1997

# Let's Plant Stars

*For Akira Sugai who moved to*
*the Andromeda Nebula in September 1997*


Akira—

Let's plant stars

on our farm!


Throw away the street lights.

—Light-show in a farm land?

Raccoon dogs are unhappy these days.

The show destroys the dignity of night.


Throw away the street lights!

Here, real night returns.

The moon & stars jump out to you.

Now you look into the beauty of darkness.


Akira—

As long as stars, trees & animals are alive,

As long as your heart keeps wide open

With an inner light,

Lets plant stars

On our farm!


Throw away numerals, watches & tomorrow,

Akira—

Let's plant stars

On our farm!

# In The Next Life I Will Be

Wiping the windowpanes of my humble shack,
A dirty dust cloth, in my hand,
Endless blue sky over my head.

At the forest edge
Where narcissus are already in all their glory,
Where wild boars bite off various trees' roots every so often,
Where I stand, piss and murmur.

> In the next life I will be a dust cloth
> Lapiz lazuli colored.

> As a dust cloth, making myself dirty
> I clean up windowpanes, kitchens and toilets,
> And I also wipe out discrimination and wars.

> If ever the world really exists
> I start polishing it from my tiny corner.
> If ever eternity really exists
> I make it brilliant at every moment.

> The more I work, the more I become
> Pure lapiz lazuli color
> Just like today's sky.

> Ten days after winter solstice
> The mother sun is shining bright.

All of a sudden, a gust of north wind
Blows the dead leaves from the trees.

Look, something coming down!
With our luminous star behind
Red wings flutter.

What is that? Hawk? Flying goblin? UFO?
Wow! On the palm of my hand
I catch the monster—
A withered red leaf of oak.

Living in the flower garden of the sun's red corona,
Biting off the rainbow's roots forever
Someone murmurs

In the next life I will be . . .

# Fine Blue Sky Over Yoshino River

Fine blue sky over Yoshino River.
Fiddler crab invites you to water.
Skylark sings high in the air.
Clouds float over your head.

If they build a huge dam here,
As the rumor goes,
I'm afraid
The sky of the twenty-first century
Won't visit Yoshino River.

If they build the dam,
I'm afraid
The concrete wall might bring with it

Hatred, anger,
Flood, drought, starvation,
Discrimination, war.

Nursing many forms of life
You, Yoshino River
Flow, flow in peace
Sing, sing your song of love
Play, play your beautiful music of landscape
Until the last day of the universe & the eternal!

Fine blue sky over Yoshino River.
Fiddler crab invites you to water.

Skylark sings high in the air.
Clouds float over your head.

Yes, river is blood.
Yes, river is light.
Yes, river is god.

Fine blue sky over Yoshino River today.

# Midway Through Space Travel

Midway through space travel
I stop casually
In woods of Ezo spruce. Quercus dentata & grizzly bear
Under the September sky of Planet Earth.

> The fruits of wild grape & silver vine
> Are blue & hard yet.
> Several peacock butterflies
> Sail around my shadow.

> The rain shadow is gone.
> In a car's furrow on a dirt road
> There lie in peace
> A frog & a blue-green snake
> Side by side.

A frog is eaten by a snake,
A snake is eaten by a car.
A car is eaten by iron rust.
Rust is eaten by the air.
Air is eaten by a frog.
Frog is eaten by a snake.
Snake is eaten by . . .

> The undergrowth of the woods
> Is covered with a kind of tall grass.
> The grass is covered with
> Royal-purple, enigmatic flowers.

Look . . . a bumblebee is eaten
By a monkshood flower, I thought.
But . . . the bee, full of pollen,
Flies to the beyond of the Universe.

1998  *Mt. Sword Hokkaido, Japan*

# I Look Up at Chomolungma
# from Kathmandu Valley

5 cm a year
Indian subcontinent
Thrusts upon Eurasia plate.

9 cm a year
Pacific Plate submerges
Underneath the Japan Deep.

300,000 km a second
The arrow of Cupid
Hits your heart.

With a huge sickle
Death god will harvest
Your neck, your life
Anytime, even right now.

I want to take a nap
At the top of Chomolungma
Someday.

JANUARY 1999

# My Dear Sister

On a dirt road passing through a jungle
Our Safari Jeep stops suddenly.
In a sandy spot, eight meters away,
Shiny black and gold stripes all over her body

Bengal tiger.
Smaller head & face — sure, a female.
Quite big belly — must be pregnant.

Hi, tiger, why are you here?
Why don't you dash into the jungle?
Why don't you jump over the jeep?
Why don't you kick away the cameras?
Time stops. I hear my heart beating as the tiger's.

Out of the ring of silence —unseen
Somehow the tiger slips into the jungle
Leaving no sound, no shadow.

After the safari people share their sighs & smiles
The jeep starts running again,
Leaving on the sand
The tiger's footprints & my broken heart.

FEBRUARY 1999 *Chitwan, Nepal*

# No More

I eat cow meat.
I eat bullfrog's meat.
I eat eel which eats bullfrog.
I dream eating man who eats eel
which eats bullfrog.

Me, a man eater, they say.
Now I eat the figure 1.
I eat 10 which eats 1.
I eat 100 which eats 10 which eats 1.
I eat 1000 which eats 100 which eats 10
which eats 1.
I eat 1000, 10,000, 100,000,000
infinity, naught.

Me, a man of straw.
I eat myself into no being.
As no being I eat myself.
As no being I, I, I . . .

Here & there
you hear
        "No More"
Bullfrogs sing
        "No More"
The long night of the rainy season sings
        "No More"

JUNE 1999 *Soma, Japan*

# Chuck

Chuck Dockham.
Born in Wyoming. Plumber. Zen Buddhist.
Once a lovely boy. A bright old man.
Now carrying cancer in his
                    pancreas stomach & intestine.
He wades "the River of No Return."

On an autumn day, years ago
I visited him in the foothills of Sierra Nevada.
    "Last night a black bear stood near the kitchen.
With a club I drove away the bear."
    "Great! Do you know the bear's name?"
    "No!"
    "I know. His name is Chuck."

Now he wades "the River of No Return."
From here, the west fringe of the Pacific
San Francisco lies due east.
To catch Chuck, how many days
I must swim to cross the ocean?
And I wonder — is "the River of No Return"
Wider than the Pacific?
The sea is high today.
One after another the swells from California
Reach the beach where I stand.

    The swells . . .
    Straight like Chuck

Vigorous like Chuck
Serious like Chuck
Capricious like Chuck
Big dopey eyes like Chuck

Hi Chuck, don't forget
Your bear's name is Chuck.

# Bye Bye September

Swallow wants to go back to the south.
Dragonfly wants to go back to her nymph.
Pampas grass wants to go back to its seed.
Orion wants to go back to winter night.
The sea wants to go back to the full moon.

> Now camping on a hospital bed.
> With his right wrist &
> Left knee fractured.

Nanao wants

> To go back
> To desert

Bye Bye
September.

# Strange, Strange

Each woman is a beauty,
Why do we need Miss Universe?

Each person is a treasure for his nation & for the world.
Why do we need the National Living Treasure?

Each mountain is wonderful.
Why do we need One Hundred Great Mountains of Japan?

Everything on earth is the sun's heritage.
Why do we need the World Natural Heritage Parks?

The sun can live Ten Billion years.
How long Japan will survive?
Nobody knows.

In the public construction enterprise
Somebody makes big money & breaks down the earth.
Why do you call it public?

Stone age Japanese never know Atomic Energy.
Now nuclear power plants are
Poisoning modern Japan to a slow death.

NOVEMBER 20, 1999 *Leaving hospital*

# Ape Man

Japanese cranes are dancing
On the snowy plain of Hokkaido
Steller's sea eagles are dancing
On the icy Okhotsk,
Ezo wolves are dancing
In the frozen wetland of Sapporo.

Every summer night
Charmed with gorgeously illuminated
Station building of Sapporo
Crane flies & ape men congregate.

"The train for 18th century Hokkaido
Is leaving 19:00, on platform 20.
You need a visa from Tokugawa shogunate."

In the concourse
A middle aged ape lady is fascinated
To look up at the sky news flash.

In the waiting room
An old ape gentleman tired of
The sports newspaper yawns secretly.

A young ape lady with a heavily decorated face,
Is looking into the bathroom mirror,
Mumbling and smiling.

In the underground hall, teen ape kids
Eat hamburgers, sip coffee &
Puff tobacco smoke.

Wave after wave of the ape men
Who want to hurry back to their sweet homes,
Run up & up to platform 1

Somewhere on platform 2,
A couple of young apes are fighting & giggling.

On platform 3,
Humbler apes are sending off
A VIP ape with "Banzai" three times.

Every summer night
At the station building of Sapporo
Numberless ape men who are
Stronger than the Ainu
Stronger than the grizzly
Stronger than the devil,
Congregate, & celebrate
Their great achievement.

"The train for 21st century
Is leaving at 22:00, on platform 23.
You need a visa from Heaven's governor."

Japanese cranes are dancing
On the snowy plain of Hokkaido.
Steller's sea eagles are dancing
On the icy Okhotsk.
Ezo wolves are dancing
In the frozen wetland of Sapporo.

*Ezo wolf became extinct at end of the 19th century.*

# What Shall I Do

Nothing in the universe, just void!

Yes! I humbly mumble.
At least there must be a horizontal line.

Beyond the horizontal line
There must be the slowly rising sun.

This side of the line
Here, I'm sitting.

In between the sun & myself
Venus is already up,
Luminosity minus 4 degrees.

Following the golden planet
Here comes
Age 27th, red brown colored
Thinly nailed moon.

Rendezvous—the moon & Venus
5AM, Feb 3rd, 2000.

What shall I do
On such an occasion?

# Garden

Somewhere in the solar system
Somewhere on the water planet
Around 19 degrees north. 155 degrees west
Here stand my friend's cabin & garden.

This is my friend's garden.
My friend is myself.
Therefore this is my garden.

A shiny, pink flower raft of bougainvillea
Big fruits on the tops of coconut palm.
Numberless, tiny fruits of mango.
Green color, green taste of avocado.

Here, in the garden,
So many kinds of
Flowers, fruits, birds & stars
Whose names I don't know yet.

I pray —
This garden shouldn't be eternal.

# Birds in the Garden

Birds in the garden.
Geckos on the walls.
Me on a chair.

    Birds sing.
    Geckos sing.
    I sing.

        Birds are short-tempered.
        Geckos short-tempered.
        I'm the same.

Birds never laugh.
Geckos never laugh.
Only I laugh.

    Somewhere
    No man can hear & see
    There—birds laugh,
    Geckos laugh.

        Birds in the garden.
        Geckos on the walls.
        Me on a chair.

MARCH 2000 *Kehena beach, Hawaii*

# I Mumble Before Going to Bed

In seven minutes
> You fall asleep.

In seven hours
> You wake up.

In seven days
> You are tired of job.

In seven years
> You forget your friends.

In seventy years
> You are gone.

In seven hundred years,
> Nobody knows you.

In seventy thousand years
> No human beings on the earth.

In seven hundred million years
> The Milky Way disappears.

In seven hundred million light years
> Somebody sleeps on your bed.

# Firefly   Here

Firefly here!
Firefly here!
Over there stinking, dirty water!
Here fresh, clean water!
Firefly here!
Firefly here!

> Are you chilly?
> Are you hungry?
> Are you thirsty for love?
> Are you tired of school?
> Don't you like your job?
> Are you short of money?
> Have you nothing to do?
> If so, come over on foot!

Firefly here!
Firefly here!
Over there stinking, dirty water!
Here fresh, clean water!
Firefly here!
Firefly here!

# You

In the next life

    You will be a robot?
        or       a spitz?
              a yellow jacket?
              a magnolia flower?
              a dinosaur?
              a mountain torrent?
              a desert highland?
              a motor car?
              a computer?
              a god?
              a Homo sapiens?

# Highlight of Spring

Without today there is no eternity.
Without me there is no universe.

Welcome back
New Leaves of beech trees,
Songs of blue winged flycatchers.
Dazzling white of magnolia flowers.

Without eternity there is no today
Without universe there is no me.

# Autobiography

In the first century
I bow the rising sun on the Pacific
Every mornings.

In the second century
Born in Noto peninsula, sea of Japan.
I eat acorn & run ahead of deer.

As a young lady
In the third century
I plant rice in wetlands of Kyushu.

Born in Hyuga
In the fourth century
I make Haniwa dolls
For the graveyard.

Born in fifth century
I'm a horse rider from Korea.

Born in the 6th century
I'm a Sue potter
at the foot of Mt. Fuji.

Born in the 7th century
I'm an Emishi, a northern barbarian
Who assasinates an army commander
From Kyoto.

Born in Kanto basin
In the 8th century
I'm a beggar poet of Manyoshu.

As a deserted child
Born in the 9th century
I was raised by wolves.
Now, I'm a lumberjack in Mt. Omine.

Born in the 10th century
I'm a gibbeted head
as an incendiary maniac.

Born in the 11th century
I'm a beautiful lady
I write many love stories.

Born in the 12th century
I'm a pirate on the East China Sea.

Born in the 13th century
I'm a country infant
Who smiles while watching the dew
On the broad leaves of taro potato
In the morning sun.

Born in the 14th century
I am a hermit
Secluding from the bloody wars.

Born in the 15th century
I'm a member of the farmer's revolt in Kaga
Which is spanning over one hundred years.

Born in the 16th century
My name is Rikyu, the master of Tea ceremony
who is given the honorable hara-kiri
by the Shogun.

Born in the 17th century
I will be killed in Hokkaido,
by the governmental army
Because I'm an Ainu.

Born in the 18th century
I'm an excellent indigo dyer of kimono
At Tokushima.

Born in the 19th century
Call me Chuji Kunisada.
They crucified me on death penalty
with twelve thrusts of spear.

Born in the 20th century
My father perished of hunger
At Guadalcanal in the South Pacific
In the WWII.
He left no ashes, no medal.

Born in the 21st century
I cook the brown rice with the internet.

# Green Breeze

How big & shiny are the leaves!
A pile of green spinach
Somebody brought
To my humble kitchen.

Spinach
Her resident registration says

"Under the ring of the sun's corona
For four billion years with stars & days
Stretching her roots in a clod of earth
And add a little bit of human sweat to it
Here comes an emerald green vegie."

Spinach.
In the stomach
Her long cherished desire
Becomes human blood
Becomes somebody's muscle
Becomes your songs
Becomes a green breeze
And flies to the unknown sky.

Spinach
The green breeze.

# Hydrangea

Hydrangea
Full blooming today.
Silver gray
Blooms on my hair & beard.

Sometime
I want to go back
To the beggar's life.
A dumb & humble beggar.

& sometime
I want to sing songs
With a loud voice.

Hydrangea
Full blooming today.

# Three Haiku

With an arrow & a bow
I shot down
Eighty-eight constellations
In my first dream of the year.


A dream—
I blow harmonica
A running rain passed.
My old aged sky.


A running rain passed.
I count stars.
Me, an eighty year old star.

# Really?

Somewhere
We, the human being
Couldn't hear any sound
There, the flowers are singing.

Somewhere
We, the human being
Couldn't see anything
There, the flowers are dancing.

Somewhere
The flowers could hear & see
There, the human sings & dances.

# Four Haiku

Fall down from the Milky Way
Right now, you
the first firefly.


You welcome
First firefly
Only today
Only tonight.


Bright enough
First firefly—
Pay no attention to the Milky Way.


Following a firefly
A shooting star fades away.

# Requiem

A spider is dead.
On the rim of the window panel.
30 mm long.
Most likely female.

In the *Tale of Genji*
The death of an honourable lady
Is not trivial.
She could be a ghost
or reborn as another person.

A spider is dead.
I wonder what is happening
In their capital
In their court.

A spider who call herself Lady Murasaki
Who wears a twelve-layered gown
Who writes a tale of spider Genji
Who writes about an environmental issue
Who writes about North-South problems.

A spider is dead.

# Water Mirror

A tiny, tiny water pond.
After a sudden shower clearing out
A sparkling pond in the mountain pass.

The pond reflects stars
reflects clouds
reflects trees
reflects birds
reflects Homo sapiens
and left nothing behind.

The tiny pond under the mountain pass.
A mirror, a water mirror.
It reflects herself
Reflects the earth
Reflects the universe.

A tiny, tiny water mirror
It sparkles
Unitl it dries out & disappears.

COLOPHON

Set in *Garamond #3*,
based on the typeface created
by Jean Jannon (1580–1658)
and modeled after the old-style faces
of Claude Garamond (1480-1561).
This version was designed in 1919
by Morris Fuller Benton
& Thomas Maitland Cleland,
and originally released by
American Type Founders (ATF).

*Bye Bye Nanao Sakaki!*